SPECIAL CAMPAIGN SERIES. No. 15

NAPOLEON'S CAMPAIGNS IN ITALY

1796–1797 and 1800

BY

BRIGADIER-GENERAL R. G. BURTON

"Above all, for Empire and Greatness, it importeth most that a Nation do profess arms as their principal honour, study and occupation."   FRANCIS BACON.

LONDON
GEORGE ALLEN & UNWIN LTD
MUSEUM STREET

THE SPECIAL CAMPAIGN SERIES

*Crown 8vo, cloth, copiously supplied with Maps and Plans.
Price 7s. 6d. net each.*

FIRST PUBLISHED IN 1912
SECOND IMPRESSION 1931

Printed by The Riverside Press Limited, Edinburgh

PREFACE

THE historian Gibbon tells us that "war and the administration of affairs are the principal subjects of history." In the opening campaign of Napoleon Bonaparte we see the conduct of events by a master of both. Especially instructive to the soldier is the first series of operations conducted by the greatest master of the art of war, whose very name sounds like a trumpet-call, and whose genius illuminates one of the most lurid and marvellous epochs in the history of the world.

In the Middle Ages and until the advent of Napoleon, the art of war as exemplified in the campaigns of Alexander and Cæsar had been neglected or forgotten. War had become a pageant, a stately ceremonial, governed by none of those logical principles which are based on the foundations of nature and of reason. It had degenerated into a series of manœuvres, frequently carried out to avoid combat, while lengthy sieges and the occupation of towns and territory were regarded as the objects of strategy, to the neglect of the true and proper object—the destruction of the enemy's armed forces.

It fell to Napoleon Bonaparte to deduce from the experience of history and to illustrate in the practice of war the whole art of military operations, based on immutable principles, and exemplified in the annals of the world.

The first campaign in which he exercised supreme command consequently marks the opening of an epoch in the art of war, and serves as a lasting example to those who would scale the glittering pinnacle of military fame. Had his career ended at Rivoli, this campaign alone would have sufficed to entitle him to that deathless fame of which he said : " I hold the immortality of the soul to be the remembrance we leave behind us in the minds of men This thought is an inspiring one. It were better never to have lived at all than to leave no trace of one's existence behind."

CONTENTS

PART I—1796-1797

CHAPTER I

CHAPTER II

CHAPTER III

CHAPTER IV

CHAPTER V

CHAPTER VI

CHAPTER VII

CHAPTER VIII

CHAPTER IX

PART II

THE CAMPAIGN OF MARENGO, 1800

CHAPTER I

CHAPTER II

The Great St Bernard—March of the Advanced
Guard—The Fort of Bard—Napoleon crosses the
Alps—Comments

CHAPTER III

Napoleon reviews the Situation—The French Ad-
vance—Movements of Melas—The Advance to Milan
—Fall of Genoa—The Conquest of Lombardy—The
Battle of Montebello—Dispositions of the French—
Comments

CHAPTER IV

Preliminary Movements—Battle of Marengo—Results of the Campaign—Comments

MAPS AND PLANS

In Pocket—

General Map of Campaign—First Campaign, 1796-97
—Invasion of Germany, 1797—Battle of Marengo

In Text—

Napoleon's Campaigns in Italy

PART I

1796-1797

CHAPTER I

CHARACTER OF THE COUNTRY AND OPPOSING FORCES

Theatre of Operations—Character of the opposing Forces—The
French Army—French Commanders—Napoleon Bonaparte
—Massena—Other Commanders—The Austrian Army—
Austrian Generals — Clausewitz' Comparison between
Napoleon and Beaulieu—The Piedmontese Army

THE theatre of operations in Italy in 1796 lay between two
great mountain ranges in country drained by the Po and
Theatre of   its tributaries which, fed by melting snows,
Operations   descend from the lofty lacustrine regions of
the Alps in the north, and from the lesser range of the
Apennines in the south. Swollen by these many waters,
the Po flows eastward through fertile plains to empty
itself into the Adriatic Sea. Beyond the Po, in Venetian
territory, the considerable streams of the Adige, the
Brenta, and the Piave have their own terminations in
the Adriatic. It will be seen, then, that the course of the
rivers that influenced the campaign was north and south,
but the Po, running almost due east from its source to the
west of Turin, was parallel to the general line of operations.

A   I

Fed by the melting of the snows, these rivers roll in turbid floods across the plains, or in lesser streams according to the season of the year. At times and in places they are fordable; generally they are passable only by bridges and boats; and Napoleon, having no pontoon train, frequently found in them formidable obstacles, as will be seen during the course of this narrative.

The mountain slopes rise abruptly from this low-lying country, the whole of which is a level plain of wonderful richness and fertility, thickly populated and containing many large and wealthy cities.

The narrow strip of coast between the Maritime Alps, the Apennines, and the sea, formerly known as Liguria, is entirely mountainous, occupied by offshoots from the main ranges, which descend to the Mediterranean coast. The mountain slopes are fertile; the valleys, traversed only by rushing torrents which cannot assume any considerable size in so short a course, are cultivated and occupied by villages. The northern Apennines have some lofty peaks, rising to a height of seven thousand feet above the sea.

The roads in those days were neither as numerous nor as good as they are in our time. At the opening of the campaign the main line of communication for the French was the coastal road from Genoa to Nice, narrow and rugged in places, situated unfavourably in prolongation of their left flank, and under fire of ships which had command of the sea. The Apennines were traversed by some difficult roads and a number of paths. In the plains of Piedmont and Lombardy were good roads connecting the principal towns, as well as navigable rivers. The lines of communication of the Austrians were therefore in no way difficult, and the rich plains which they traversed rendered supply a comparatively easy matter.

Politically, the area of operations was divided into various states and principalities. There was the kingdom of Piedmont; Lombardy; the dukedoms of Parma and Modena; the states of Genoa and Venice, nominally republics, in reality oligarchies whose despotism, like that of many so-called democratic governments, was, if possible, more tyrannical than the autocracies of unlimited monarchies; and the states over which the Pope had both spiritual and temporal power. The inhabitants were mainly neutral, their sympathies varying with the changing fortunes of war, but many were inspired by the new ideas propagated throughout Europe by the French Revolution.

For a full comprehension of the operations of war it is necessary to have some knowledge of the opposing forces, Character of their strength, their organisation, their train-
the opposing ing and their armament. More than this,
Forces the psychology and the characteristics of the peoples of which armies are composed exercise a great influence on the course of events; whilst perhaps more important than all is the character of the higher leaders; for, as Von Moltke said, " in war everything is uncertain from the beginning except the amount of will-power and energy with which the Commander-in-Chief himself is endowed."

Napoleon's Army of Italy was formed from the French National Guard, called into being by the National As-
The French sembly in 1792. This National Guard was a
Army force of two or three million citizens who, although armed only with pikes, furnished the armies of the Revolution. Obligatory service was established for all males between the ages of eighteen and forty, and systematic conscription was instituted in 1793, when the methods of Carnot, the great Minister of War, were enforced by the Committee of Public Safety. By this means the Republic was able to put 600,000 men into the field.

The troops were organised by the genius of Carnot, the
" organiser of victory," who clothed, fed, and drilled the
conscripts of 1798. He devised the new tactics. Under
his administration not seniority, birth nor influence were
standards of rank and command, but merit only. He it
was who brought into being the galaxy of great soldiers
who adorn the annals of the Napoleonic epoch. To this,
no doubt, the high standard of military efficiency attained
at that period was mainly due ; and in this connection it is
noteworthy that Machiavelli, in his " Art of War," tells
us that " the decline of military skill in Rome dates from
the time when science and talent were despised, and only
those gained distinction who knew how to please the
authorities." All history bears out the truth of this observation.

The Army of Italy was organised in demi-brigades of
battle, each some 3000 strong, and light demi-brigades of
from 1000 to 1500 men. Four demi-brigades formed a
division of infantry. The reserve divisions were less—
of from 3000 to 4000 men. The cavalry was organised in
divisions of five regiments each. The guns were at first
attached to battalions, and were mostly 12-pounders,
having a range of some 1500 yards, or 500 yards with
case shot. There were three or four guns per thousand
men, two accompanying the battalion and one or two being
in reserve. In 1796 they were mostly withdrawn from
battalions and formed into batteries.

The French infantry were armed with a flint-gun, most
effective at about 180 yards, and ranging up to 500 yards.
Trained men fired two rounds a minute. Each man carried
fifty rounds, and the artillery waggons as many more.

The French soldiery, inspired by the enthusiasm of the
new republican era, were splendid, and almost invincible
as long as they believed themselves to be so. The infantry

was the best in Europe and contained the finest elements in the army ; sons of old families were proud to serve in the ranks, and malefactors were excluded ; but the cavalry was much inferior to that of the Austrians until Napoleon took it in hand.

French armies marched light, and lived on the country by requisition, thus obviating the necessity of a lengthy supply train or of magazines. Each man carried three or four days' supplies, and double that amount was on regimental transport. A few waggons followed with ammunition, medical supplies, and biscuits. For the rest, troops lived on the land.

The French endured fatigue and privation with wonderful constancy. They were active and enterprising, of superior intelligence, and most susceptible to appeals to vanity and the love of glory, with which Napoleon's proclamations were well calculated to inspire them. They knew well how to adapt themselves to ground, and to take advantage of natural features. In the early days of the Revolution custom and drill-books were cast aside, and the stiff and cumbrous order of battle previously in vogue gave place to more flexible formations. Their fighting formations, covered by clouds of skirmishers, were far more mobile than those of their opponents, and their sharpshooters were thus able to harass the more immobile Austrians. Napoleon taught co-operation between infantry and artillery, and won the battle of Lodi largely by the skilful handling of his guns.

The commissioned ranks of the army had also undergone a change. Hundreds of Royalist officers had been French removed, imprisoned and guillotined, and Commanders younger men had come to the front. This regeneration of their leaders undoubtedly contributed largely to the efficiency of the troops.

Napoleon Bonaparte, who had boundless physical and mental energy, was in 1796 under twenty-seven years of age. He had already distinguished himself at the siege of Toulon, and in the suppression of the Sections of Paris, when he cleared the streets with the famous " whiff of grape-shot." He had made a special study of Italy as a theatre of war, and had been with the Army of Italy in 1794, and such success as had been met with was greatly due to his plans which ultimately developed into the famous Campaign of Italy.

Napoleon Bonaparte

The relations of armies to ground and the use of the map and compass, which had been forgotten, were revived by him. He had a classical education, and in the history of past campaigns had studied the causes of success and failure, and had learned that certain causes always produce certain effects. Like Hadrian he " possessed the various talents of the soldier, the statesman, and the scholar."

After the battle of Lodi, Berthier wrote to General Clarke, plenipotentiary of the Republic :

" The military genius of Bonaparte, the precision and clarity of his ideas, his character as audacious and enterprising as it is cool in execution, has given us the means of carrying out one of the finest campaigns of which history has ever furnished an example."

At this time, it is recorded, his personal appearance had nothing of dignity about it. The Greek features and the commanding and awe-inspiring bearing were subsequently developed.

" Owing to his thinness his features were almost ugly in their sharpness ; his walk was unsteady, his clothes neglected, his appearance produced on the whole an unfavourable impression and was in no way imposing ; but

in spite of his apparent bodily weakness he was tough and
sinewy, and from under his deep forehead there flashed,
despite his sallow face, the eyes of genius, deep-seated, large,
and of a greyish-blue colour, and before their glance and
the words of authority that issued from his thin, pale lips,
all bowed down." [1]

He had hitherto acted a subordinate part, but was now
to appear on a great stage, where his genius would carry
all before it ; for, although he had able subordinates, his
was the brain to conceive and the hand to execute.   Well
versed in the theory of the art of war, he had also the
ability to reduce it to bold and successful practice.

One of the greatest figures of an epoch so fertile in
military genius was Massena, who, said Napoleon, " had
an audacity and a *coup-d'œil* which I have seen
in him alone " ; a man made by character for
authority and command, of whom Pasquier, who knew all the
great commanders of his time, said : " A man born for war,
possessing genius and endowed with all the qualities which
must lead to victory, the next greatest to Napoleon."

Massena

Massena, being an Italian, was acquainted with the
language and the theatre of operations, and had fought
the campaign and gained the victory of Loano in 1795.
His character, and the spirit with which he led the French
soldiers to victory, perhaps stands out more clearly in the
following passage from the French of Edouard Gachot [2] :—

" Massena often visited the advanced posts.   From the
heights he observed the enemy's lines, and noted the
marches of the Austro-Sardinians on the frontiers of Piedmont.   His cloak covered with snow, he ate in the bivouac
the frozen bread of the soldier ; he reanimated failing

---

[1] " Napoleon as a General."   By Count Yorck von Wartenburg.
[2] " The Campaign in Italy."   By Edouard Gachot.

courage ; he recalled to the men the grandeur of sacrifice accomplished in the service of France. And almost always the invocation of the duties due to the flag, whatever the weather or the hour, revived energies which one thought dead; even those of men who suffered from hunger but acclaimed Massena in recommending patience and patriotism as the infallible remedies against all ills."

There was Augereau, possessed of great character, courage, firmness and activity, having the *habitude de la* Other *guerre*, and beloved by his soldiers ; Serurier, Commanders a veteran of commanding presence and wide experience ; Berthier, a model Chief of the Staff, possessing a capacity for infinite labour, although he did not learn the art of war in twenty campaigns. There were numbers of other brave and skilful officers — Laharpe, Marmont, Junot, Joubert, Lannes, Joachim Murat, all names that live in history, and the gallant and invincible Rampon, of whose deeds we shall soon hear. Some were at first inclined to oppose the youthful general who had been placed over them, but all quickly bowed to his inflexible will.

At the outbreak of the French Revolution, the establishment of the Austrian army was about 300,000 men— The Austrian including 240,000 infantry and 40,000 cavalry, Army recruited by conscription based on the territorial system. The long-service system was in force, and in 1796 the army consisted almost entirely of veterans, it being held that only a veteran of forty possessed the skill, experience, and endurance requisite for campaigning. The army thus contained thousands of useless men past their prime, and up to ten years' service men were classed as recruits.

Infantry regiments were composed of four battalions each, and battalions of six companies, the grenadier companies having the finest and strongest men. Infantry of the line carried a muzzle-loading flint-gun, ranging up to 300 yards; light infantry a smaller gun, ranging up to 200 yards. Each man carried sixty rounds of ammunition. The normal rate of marching was very slow. The usual method of attack was in lines of battalions, battalions being divided into three sections. Fire was by battalion or section salvoes, always in close formation. Outpost duties, skirmishing, and reconnaissance were the work of light infantry and irregulars, such as the Austrian hussars and the Tyrolese sharp-shooters.

In 1796 the Archduke Charles said : " Well-drilled and compact infantry, advancing in close formation under the protection of their guns, can never be stopped by scattered skirmishers. Sharp-shooting and skirmishing cost lives and decide nothing. . . . It would be unpardonable if we were to give up the advantages of our training and discipline for the sake of copying the enemy in methods of fighting to which they are only driven as a necessity by their poor organisation."

He soon had cause to modify this opinion, which is interesting and instructive as showing the ideas prevalent in military systems of the old type. It must at the same time be borne in mind that formations and methods of fighting should be adapted to the nature and characteristics of peoples and their opponents ; the craze for uniformity and imitation, so prevalent in most military systems, is indicative of a narrow type of mind.

The Austrian army presented a magnificent and imposing spectacle. Their cavalry were well-mounted and fine horsemen. In the days of Maria Theresa their artillery had been the best in Europe. The 12-pounder gun, most commonly in use, had a range of 1500 yards. At the opening of the war in Italy the tactical organisation was the same as in the Seven Years' War—in corps, divisions, and brigades.   War was with the Austrians a slow and methodical operation, not aiming primarily at the destruction of the enemy's armed forces.   The conquest of a province, the reduction of a fortress, or the repulse of a relieving force were considered satisfactory results of a campaign, and conflict was rather evaded by manœuvre. Wars were in fact more wars of position than of movement. Armies lived on their magazines, not on the country, and a general seldom ventured more than five marches from depots, and moved about seven or eight miles a day.   The true object of war had been forgotten, although enunciated some centuries previously by Machiavelli in his " Art of War " : " The object of every war is to vanquish the enemy on the field of battle."

The Austrian soldiers were brave and could bear heavy losses ; but they performed their duties mechanically.   In light infantry tactics and in mountain warfare they were far inferior to the French.   They could not adapt themselves to the ground.   Instead of occupying heights, they massed at the foot of them.   They generally fought on the defensive, dividing their forces, which were thus weak everywhere.   Manœuvring in masses opposed to the French skirmishers, they were soon rendered helpless and immobile. Their national weakness was the fear of being outflanked or turned, an apprehension which disconcerted their plans at a time when victory demanded only an advance.

Austrian generals were disciplined by rule, and accus-
Austrian   tomed to execute the letter of an order.   In
Commanders proportion as rank descended, conduct became more mechanical, until the private soldier was a mere automaton.

The Austrian army was, at the opening of the campaign, commanded by Beaulieu, between whom and Napoleon the following comparison has been drawn by Clausewitz :—

"Bonaparte was twenty-seven years old; Beaulieu, seventy-two. The first was about to inaugurate a **Comparison** brilliant career in which by audacity and **between** temerity he could gain everything and had **Napoleon and** nothing to lose; the other was at the end of **Beaulieu** his. Bonaparte had a strong classical education, and the great events of the history of the world had passed in panorama before his eyes; Beaulieu was formed by sixty years of official pedantry, most certain to deprive him of intelligence and character. Bonaparte could consider the masters of France his equals, those who owed their existence to his sword on the 13th Vendémiaire. Beaulieu was the servant of an ancient imperial house, and the instrument of a stupid and ponderous Aulic Council. Bonaparte knew the Apennines, as he had played there an important rôle in the campaign of 1794; for Beaulieu mountains and their warfare were entirely new things. In short, Beaulieu was not a mediocre man; he had not only fought with distinction in the Low Countries, to which he owed the honour of being called to this command; he was not wanting in energy, and he was far above the officers of his time; but that was not sufficient in the present case. That did not even suffice to win him the confidence of his army; it appears, on the contrary, that indiscipline arose after his arrival. It was quite otherwise on the side of Bonaparte."

In command of the Austrian divisions were Argenteau, a man of no account, of whom Drake, the British agent, wrote, " The miserable Argenteau is only fit to make war in the boudoirs of women"; the brave and enterprising Illyrian Wukassovich, and Roccavina, who was wounded early in the campaign. Allied with the Austrian army were the Piedmontese, commanded by Colli, an Austrian in the service of Victor Amadeus, King of Sardinia, whose territories included Piedmont. Quasdanovich, Lusignan, Liptay and Ocskay were brave leaders whom we shall meet with in this campaign.

The Piedmontese resembled the French more than their allies in general characteristics, but they had rusted in **The** forty years of peace. The troops were at first **Piedmontese** enthusiastic, and burning to avenge the defeat **Army** of Loano, but their ardour was extinguished under inferior leaders. Victor Amadeus had not more than 30,000 effective men, and timid counsels prevailed in political circles at Turin. By nature the Piedmontese were warlike, obedient, inured to fatigue, intelligent, and courageous, and their corps had distinguished itself at Toulon. The excellence of their artillery was due to de Antoni, well known in Europe; their artillery school was equal to the best in Europe, and the arsenal of Turin was the most perfect and complete. Their cavalry was too heavy; their light troops, mountaineers of Nice and Tenda, were excellent.

CHAPTER II

OPENING OF THE CAMPAIGN

General Situation—Napoleon Bonaparte appointed to Command
—Condition of the French Army—Supplies—Situation of
opposing Forces—Position of the French—Position of the
Allies—Intelligence—Austrian Plans—Napoleon's Plans—
The Campaign begins—Defence of Monte Legino—Movements of the French—Napoleon's Orders, 11th April—Cause
and Effect—The Battle of Montenotte—Operation Orders—
Battle of Millesimo—Battle of Dego—Defeat of the Piedmontese—Submission of Piedmont—Manifesto to the Army
of Italy—Comments

In the year 1795 the Austrian Archduke Charles had conducted a brilliant campaign against the French generals,
General   Moreau and Jourdan, on the Rhine; but the
Situation   Austrians and Piedmontese had suffered a
set-back in Italy, having been defeated by Massena
at the battle of Loano, which secured Liguria to the
French.

The general plan of the French Directory in 1796 was
for Moreau and Jourdan with 180,000 men in Germany to
drive back the Archduke Charles from the Rhine, and march
on Vienna; Kellermann, stationed on the Western Alps,
was to hold the Duke of Aosta who, with headquarters at
Turin, commanded an army at the foot of those mountains;
and the Army of Italy, which held the Apennines and the
country between them and the sea, was to conquer
Lombardy.

13

In February 1796 General Scherer, in resigning command of the Army of Italy, wrote to the Directory :

Napoleon Bonaparte appointed to Command   " I conjure you, I beg you to send a general who has more resources and ability than I have, for I declare that I am incapable of charging myself, in these circumstances, with the burthen of command."

In pursuance of the plan of the French Government, Napoleon Bonaparte was appointed to command the Army of Italy. He had already distinguished himself as an officer of artillery at Toulon ; he had been at Nice, Genoa, and on the Apennines in 1794, and his plans for the invasion of Italy had been laid before the War Minister. Finally, his suppression of the Sections of Paris had confirmed his reputation with the French Government, and had assured his future advancement. These considerations led to his appointment to command the army that was to retrieve the fortunes of the republic in Northern Italy.

On the 26th March 1796, Napoleon Bonaparte arrived at Nice to take command of the army, which was scattered in detachments as far as Genoa, in the mountains and along the strip of land between the Apennines and the sea. In the preceding year the troops under Massena and Augereau had met with some success, and had gained a signal victory at Loano, which had given them the summits of the Apennines ; but they were now almost immobilised in cantonments for want of supplies of food, clothing, and money. The war-worn and weary soldiers were, however, soon inspired with fresh life and energy by the genius of the young commander, who addressed them in stirring words :

" Soldiers ! You are naked and ill-fed; the Government owes you much but can give you nothing. Your patience, your valour among these rocks have been admirable, but they bring you no glory ; not a ray falls upon you. I will lead you into the most fertile plains on earth. You shall conquer rich provinces and great cities ; there you will find wealth and honour. Soldiers of Italy ! Will you be wanting in courage or endurance ? "

Although no doubt many of the soldiers were ill-clothed and ill-fed, barefooted and suffering from the rigours of Condition of winter on the Apennines, it is probable that the French the army was as a whole not in as bad a state Army as has been frequently represented. In some of the advanced posts, where the winter had been most severe, the men had neither clothes nor shoes. They wrapped themselves in pieces torn from tents, or in woollen coverings stolen from the peasants. Some of the officers were dressed in goatskins. There were to be seen in the ranks grenadiers of horrible appearance, who had not washed for two years. In this miserable state of affairs it is not surprising that there was much pillage and some insubordination. But we are told that on the 21st March the Army of Italy at length had its cadres and regiments completed. There remained but few old officers, veterans of the monarchy. The young men were or promised to be brave. The non-commissioned officers were found on inspection to be active and well trained. The soldiers of Loano charged and fired well ; and, long-tried by privations, tired of inaction, they thirsted for glory and asked only to quit the mountains, and to be led into the fertile plains below.

On the 29th March 1796, General Bonaparte inspected the troops at Nice, and was well satisfied with their appearance. At Albenga on the 6th April he published in an order the expression of his satisfaction in seeing the turn-out, dress and arms of the men, and the discipline, training, good spirits and ardour of the two demi-brigades which he inspected there.

But no doubt the effect of his presence and his measures had already made itself felt. For on assuming command Supplies for his first care was to see to the supply of the the Army troops with arms, food, clothing and transport. Provisions had been pouring in for some time, although Napoleon wrote to Massena on the 30th March :

" Your division has been for two months without meat, without pay, and often without bread. This painful situation affects me deeply ; already the left, the centre, and the coast have good bread, fresh meat five days out of ten, and have received portion of their pay. I have taken measures to have your division supplied with good bread, with meat five days out of ten, and with brandy whenever circumstances admit of it. I am sending cattle to your division independently of several employés who have been despatched by the meat purveyor to purchase on the spot where you are. I hope, citizen general, that in a few days the lot of your soldiers will be ameliorated ; tell them that when they suffer it is physically impossible that they should be better off."

The army was still in want of artillery. Napoleon obtained thirty-six pieces from the arsenals at Antibes and Toulouse and distributed them among the various divisions.

On the 11th April Napoleon arrived at Savona, where he met Massena. By dint of his exertion during the short time that had elapsed since he assumed command he had organised his army, which was now ready to undertake active operations. He had already been able to write to the Directory: "Our commissariat is assured for a month; our communications are secure."

In the spring of 1796 the opposing forces faced each other along the passes of the Apennines, the French with 47,000 Situation of men occupying the line from the Col di Tenda opposing to Voltri, with 18,000 in reserve on the coast; Forces the allied Austrians and Piedmontese, some 57,000 strong, held the line Coni, Mondovi, Ceva and eastward to the Bochetta Pass, north of Genoa. Genoa was nominally neutral but in fact had favoured the allies, largely, no doubt, under pressure of the British fleet under Nelson, who, however, quitted Genoa for Naples on the 30th March.

The principal passes over the Apennines were the Col di Tenda, a steep and rugged defile leading from Nice to Coni, where the Piedmontese occupied the fortress; and the Bochetta between Genoa and Novi on the Austrian left. There were also difficult paths over the mountains leading into Piedmont from Voltri, Savona, Loano, and Oneglia to Ceva.

Massena commanded the two divisions of the advanced guard which, under Laharpe and Meynier respectively, Position of had their headquarters at Savona and Finale. the French Augereau, commanding the 3rd Division, was at Loano in support of Serurier, who was at the pass of Ormea with 7000 men; while Stengel and Kilmaine commanded the cavalry, 2500 strong, posted on the line of communications which lay along the coast road from Genoa to Nice, then a rough, difficult and narrow way, exposed to the guns of the British cruisers. The French left under Garnier at first extended as far as Isola, in communication with Kellermann's Army of the Alps, but as the operations developed these troops were drawn in to guard the line of communications.

B

The most important points were, at the opening of the campaign, guarded by Serurier, by Macquard, who commanded 3000 men on the Col di Tenda, and by Colonel Rampon, who held with a detachment the head of the gorge at Monte Legino, on the road from Savona to Sasello. Voltri, the key of the roads to Alessandria and Acqui was held by a detachment regarding which Napoleon wrote to Massena on the 28th March :

" You will keep only 3000 men on the heights of Voltri ; take care to ensure their communications with Savona ; do nothing to make the enemy think that we intend to assume the offensive."

To this Massena replied next day :

" There is no news from the advanced guard. The two divisions occupy, the first from Monte Legino to Toviano; the second from Seigno to Melogno. The principal posts in the first are Monte Legino, Cadibona, and Baracon. In the second, Saint Jacques and Settipani. The enemy being reinforced at Dego, I sent out a reconnaissance in force under Brigadier-General Menard. All the enemy's advanced posts were driven back."

The allies were widely distributed. On the right Colli with 25,000 Piedmontese had his headquarters at Ceva, Position of where there was an intrenched camp and the Allies where he could watch the descents from both the Col di Tenda and the pass of Ormea, which looked down on the valley of the Tanaro. His lines of communication with Turin were by roads through Alba, Cherasco, and Fossano.

The centre under Argenteau, who had 9000 men, was at

Dego and Sasello, forty miles east of Ceva, with which it was connected by small detachments. Beaulieu, the Commander-in-Chief, was twenty-five miles farther west, above the Bochetta, on the road from Alessandria to Genoa.

The French were well served with intelligence by their spies, who were systematically organised by their chief, the celebrated Pico. Between the 5th and 7th April, Pico gave a detailed account of the movements and position of the Austrians, whose reinforcement at the Bochetta and Sasello pointed to their probable assumption of the offensive from their left flank. Indeed, Pico stated plainly that the allies were intending to drive the French from Voltri, and cut their communications with Genoa, on which place they were largely dependent for supplies.

Intelligence

The Austrian plan of campaign was in fact for Beaulieu to advance from the Bochetta and attack the French at Voltri; simultaneously Argenteau was to move from Sasello and occupy Savona. The French would thus be cut in two at Savona; their right would be destroyed; their left would be rolled up by an advance on Nice which, in view of the precarious position of their line of communication in prolongation of their left flank, would clear Liguria from end to end.

Austrian Plans

Napoleon had, on the 27th March, asked permission to march through Genoese territory and advance through the Bochetta against the Austrian left. He rightly calculated that the Government of Genoa would give this information to his opponent, who would thus be misled as to his intentions, and would act accordingly and still further weaken his already weak centre. In this he judged correctly.

Napoleon's Plans

In reality Napoleon had a very different plan, based on the axiom he propounded when he said : " The principles of war are the same as those of a siege. Fire must be concentrated on one point, and as soon as the breach is made the equilibrium is broken and the rest is nothing." He would not prolong any resistance to the Austrian attack on Voltri, as already indicated in his instructions to Massena; taking advantage of their wide dispersion and the weakness of their centre, he would concentrate his force in an attack on their centre, and, pouring his army from the Apennines like a torrent into the plains of Piedmont, he would defeat in detail the separated wings of his opponent's armies. The line selected for the advance was where the mountains are of least altitude, from Savona by way of Cadibona, Altare and Carcare into the valley of the Bormida.

In a few days Napoleon had secured an almost incredible ascendancy over his men. He left Nice on the 2nd and reached Albenga on the 4th April.

The Campaign begins

On the 8th April Colonel Rampon, " one of the bravest soldiers in the Army of Italy, adored by his grenadiers, always fortunate in his operations," was directed to carry out next day a reconnaissance with 600 out of his 1200 men in the direction of Sasello. At midnight he assembled his men on the road from Cairo to Altare.

Later in the day, 9th April, he massed his force at Monte Legino above Montenotte, commanding the valley of the Albissola and the road to Cairo, and dominating Savona, a defensive position of great strength which, before the battle of Loano, the Austrians had crowned with a redoubt. Against this post, with a view to executing his task of advancing to Savona, Argenteau marched with 2500 men on the morning of the 10th April, after driving in the French outposts at Monte-

Defence of Monte Legino

notte. Three times he attacked with fury, but the position was practically impregnable; the Austrians were on each occasion repulsed with heavy loss, the French having only some forty casualties. At nightfall Argenteau, discouraged and expecting reinforcements, withdrew and encamped out of musket-shot.

Meanwhile, on this same day, Cervoni at Voltri was holding back Beaulieu, who began his forward movement **Movements** on the 9th, and who believed that he had in **of the French** front of him the leading columns of the French army; while Laharpe with his division was climbing the southern slope of the Apennines to fall on the Austrians at Montenotte. During the night Rampon was reinforced by a battalion and three guns, and on the 11th the defenders of the redoubt were subjected only to a cannonade in the evening. That day at Savona, Napoleon heard the guns of Monte Legino.

Cervoni held his own, but, harassed by the fire of British gunboats and assailed by superior forces, he at night withdrew from Voltri, and rejoined Laharpe's division. Massena and Augereau, scaling the heights above Savona, passed by Altare, marching by Cadibona and Quiliano for the Austrian rear. Napoleon, guided by the *curé* of Cadibona, proceeded towards Altare, and issued two letters of instructions to Massena:

1. "To send Dommartin with two battalions to Montefredo. Joubert to take up a position at Altare, **Napoleon's** joining up with Laharpe's division." **Orders,** 2. "General Massena will give his orders for **11th April** Brigadier-General Menard, as soon as the order reaches him, to proceed with the troops that are at Baracon, Cadibona and Quiliano, to Altare; they will take all the cartridges they have; he will place himself

at the head of these troops and will try and cut the enemy between Carcare, Altare and Montenotte.

" Brigadier-General Joubert and General Dommartin will join him during the night when, by this diversion, the troops which have attacked Monte Legino are no longer on the offensive; headquarters will be moved to Altare.

" General Massena will inform me of his arrival at Altare, and of the movements of the enemy; he will issue all further orders which he may judge necessary for the execution of the dispositions now ordered."

Thus, while Beaulieu thought he was bearing all before him from the direction of the Bochetta, while Argenteau **Cause and** was already acclaiming victory before Monte **Effect** Legino, 36,000 Frenchmen were marching to destroy the weak Austrian centre, and thus cut them off from their allies, at the same time threatening Beaulieu's communications. The two Austrian leaders were separated from each other by an impassable ridge of mountains, over which they were unable even to communicate.

Next morning Laharpe attacked Argenteau, and was seconded by Massena, who destroyed Roccavina's brigade, **Battle of** overthrew the enemy in Montenotte, enveloped **Montenotte,** their left and rear, and took 1500 prisoners. **12th April** Rampon, issuing from Monte Legino, joined in the fight, and before ten o'clock in the morning the battle was gained. The Austrian centre was driven in, and Argenteau forced back to Dego. Beaulieu, when he heard of this defeat next day, retired in order to secure his communications.

On the day of the battle Napoleon, who accompanied Massena, arrived at Carcare, and issued orders at 2 P.M. for Massena to advance to Dego with a demi-brigade, to levy a contribution, and to collect all the mules he could find and send them to the commissary at Carcare :

"He will make some movements towards Spino where he will send some light companies to cover the line of retreat. These movements should begin at dawn. If General Dommartin arrives with his troops, he will rejoin Massena, who will give him his orders.

"General Laharpe, starting at daybreak, will advance to the heights of Cairo. At 9 o'clock in the morning he will leave no more than one battalion on those heights, and will go with the rest of his troops to Cairo, where he will levy a contribution and collect mules. (This was to watch Beaulieu.)

"General Augereau will advance at daybreak with his two last brigades and his artillery by Millesimo, Roccavilla, and Montezemo, where he will attack the enemy.

"General Joubert will move at daybreak to Castelnuovo, and try to cut up the troops at Saint Jean. Master of Montezemo, he will make good all the positions in the neighbourhood of Ceva.

"Brigadier-General Menard will remain on the heights of Biestri. If General Dommartin arrives in time, they will reunite with General Massena to execute the movements which have been ordered.

"The artillery [1] will follow the columns to which they are attached, with the exception of the 8-pounder, which is with General Joubert and should be in General Augereau's park.

"The cavalry will remain at headquarters pending further orders."

[1] There were fourteen guns distributed among the divisions of Laharpe, Meynier, and Augereau. They fought at Montenotte and Dego and were then placed under Augereau's orders for the attack on the intrenched camp at Ceva.

The result of these dispositions was that on the 18th April Augereau and Joubert attacked Provera, who was **Action at** posted at Millesimo to maintain communica- **Millesimo** tion between Colli and Argenteau, defeated him and drove him into the castle of Cosseria, to which they laid siege.

Massena arrived before Dego with one demi-brigade only, but, finding the Austrians strongly posted, wisely refrained from attacking them and remained in observation at Rochetta.

Dommartin, owing to difficulties on the march, did not arrive in time, and Menard awaited him.

This day Argenteau was at Dego ; Beaulieu, instead of concentrating, was directing some of his forces under **Battle of** Wukassovich on that place, and collecting **Dego** his main body at Acqui. Next day Provera capitulated ; Massena, who had assembled his forces, with three columns, under Joubert, Dommartin and Menard, drove the Austrians from Dego back on Acqui, after a vigorous resistance in which both sides suffered heavy losses. In the meantime Meynier's division, left to guard the communications at Dego while Massena was following the enemy, had dispersed in search of plunder ; in this disorder they were attacked by Wukassovich, detached by Beaulieu to the assistance of Argenteau, who came upon them at Sasello on the morning of the 15th, threw them into confusion, destroyed numbers, and took 500 prisoners. It required Massena's reserve to rally the fugitives on the Bormida and drive the Illyrian to Acqui.

The allies were now divided. A wedge had been driven in between them ; they were separated by thirty-eight **Defeat of the** miles of mountainous country, and it only **Piedmontese** remained to beat them in detail. Napoleon decided to attack the Piedmontese and force them to come to terms which would leave him free to deal with the Austrians, who would be inferior to him in numbers. The left division under Serurier advancing from Ormea, supported by Augereau, now attacked Colli's Piedmontese, who had occupied the strongly-intrenched camp at Ceva; while Massena held the Austrians in check between the western branch of the Bormida and the Tanaro, until relieved of this duty by Laharpe, when he moved to Mombacaro and threatened Colli's left. There he remained until the 20th April. That night by Napoleon's direction he crossed the Tanaro near Ceva, to occupy the Lesigno-Mondovi road, a movement which determined the retreat of Colli to Vicoforte, pursued by Stengel's cavalry. Here Colli made a stand against the divisions of Serurier and Massena, but his troops were finally dispersed by a cavalry charge in which Stengel lost his life. The Piedmontese, broken and dispersed, fled behind the Stura. Napoleon continued the pursuit down the valley of the Tanaro, invested Cherasco, which yielded, and drove Colli on towards Turin.

Victor Amadeus now sued for a suspension of hostilities, and on the 26th April an armistice was signed at Cherasco, Submission the headquarters of Napoleon. The fortresses of Piedmont of Coni, Tortoni and Alessandria with all their guns were given up to the French, these covering Napoleon's intended line of operations into Lombardy. The conquered territory between the Stura and Bormida was also ceded, and the French commander obtained the right of sending his couriers by Turin and Susa to Paris, shortening the distance by one half. Well might Napoleon say : "Hannibal stormed the Alps, we have turned them." In fifteen days he had passed the Apennines, pierced the centre of the allies, inflicted severe defeat on one wing of the Austrian army, and defeated and forced terms on the Piedmontese. All this with a loss of about 6000 men.

Such were the results of the most rapid warfare that Europe had beheld in modern times. Before the invader lay the most fertile plains on earth, dotted with rich and populous cities. His soldiers need no more be naked and ill-fed. They were in a land of plenty.

At this time and frequently during the course of the campaign in Italy Napoleon was obliged to adopt stern measures in suppressing the licentious and plundering habits of the French soldiery. This added greatly to his labours, and he wrote to the Directory :

" You cannot realise what my life is here; I arrive fatigued, but have to keep awake all night to settle questions of administration, and be everywhere to restore order."

And again—

" I shall establish discipline or cease to command these bandits."

But the bandits were fine soldiers. Fired by the enthusiasm of successful warfare, they were inspired to fresh deeds by their great commander, who issued another stirring manifesto :

" Soldiers ! You have in fifteen days gained six victories, taken twenty-one colours, fifty-five pieces of cannon, several fortresses, and conquered the richest part of Piedmont. You have taken 15,000 prisoners and killed or wounded more than 10,000 men.

Manifesto to the Army of Italy

" Hitherto you had fought for barren rocks, made famous by your courage but useless to your country.

To-day your services have made you the equals of the armies of Holland and the Rhine. You have won battles without guns, passed rivers without bridges, accomplished forced marches barefooted, bivouacked without brandy and often without bread. Republican phalanxes, the soldiers of liberty, could alone endure what you have endured. Soldiers ! thank you for this. A grateful country will owe her prosperity to you ; and if, as victors of Toulon, you presaged the immortal campaign of 1794, your present victories presage one still greater.

" The two armies which lately attacked you boldly are flying before you in dismay. Those who mocked at your wretchedness, and rejoiced in thought at the triumphs of your enemies, are confounded and trembling.

" But, soldiers ! you have done nothing, since there is still much for you to do. Neither Turin nor Milan is yours. The ashes of the victors of Tarquin are still trodden by the assassins of Basseville ! You were destitute of everything at the beginning of the campaign ; you have now abundant provisions.

" Numerous magazines have been taken from your enemies. The siege and field artillery have arrived. Soldiers ! France has a right to expect great things of you. Will you justify her expectation ? The greatest obstacles have been surmounted ; but there are still battles to fight, towns to take, rivers to cross. Is there one among you whose courage weakens ? Is there one who would rather return and endure patiently on the summits of the Alps and Apennines the insults of that slavish soldiery ? No, there is none such among the victors of Montenotte, of Millessimo, of Dego, and Mondovi. All are burning to carry afar the glory of the French people. All are bent on humiliating those arrogant kings who dared to entertain the thought of imposing chains upon us. All are bent on dictating a glorious peace, which shall compensate our country for her great sacrifices. All wish to take pride in saying when they return to their homes : ' I belonged to the victorious Army of Italy ! ' "

The character of Napoleon impressed itself deeply on the opening phase of the campaign. In the first place he gave his careful attention to the organisation of the commissariat and to guarding his precarious line of communication. Then followed the survey of the situation, the rapid and unerring decision, and the swiftness of execution rendered possible by careful forethought and preparation. Within a month of his arrival at Nice he had broken the enemy's centre and defeated the Piedmontese and the Austrian right wing.

Comments

Certainly he had able subordinates, but at every point we trace the work of the master-brain both in conception and execution. We note the ascendancy he had obtained over his army by force of character and a true estimate of human nature ; the submission to which he had reduced somewhat refractory subordinates, for he who was himself impatient of authority exacted the most explicit obedience from those under his command.

His strategical conceptions were due to no inborn genius, no inspiration of the moment. They were based on the immutable principles derived from a close study and consideration of military history which, says Jomini, " rightly interpreted, is the true school of war." Like Cromwell, " in things of the mind he looked for no other compulsion but that of light and reason " ; and he recognised that cause and effect are two sides of one fact.

He had no experience of war as experience is commonly understood ; but he had what is worth more, the experience gathered from the wide domain of history and the ability to apply it in practice.

Indeed, in a lifetime the ordinary soldier can have comparatively little personal experience of war, and such as he has more probably tends to limit his mental horizon and obscure his view of the wider issues of military art, unless he has also deeply studied war ; just as the general who is too near the actual scene of conflict in a battle is liable to have his attention distracted by minor issues, and his breadth of vision narrowed by what is taking place before his eyes.

Napoleon himself said : " All great leaders of ancient times, as well as those who have since followed in their footsteps, accomplished great deeds only by observing the principles of the art of war, by the correctness of their combinations and a careful weighing of means and results. They have succeeded only by adapting themselves to these principles, no matter what the boldness of their enterprises and the extent of their operations. They never ceased to make war a true science. To this extent they are our great examples, and only by imitation can we hope to emulate their deeds. The principles of the whole art of war are those which guided the great commanders whose exploits are handed down to us by history." At the same time it must be borne in mind that the lessons of history are no guides to be followed blindly and mechanically, nor are the facts in themselves of importance, but the knowledge we derive from them. Wisdom, however, does not consist in the mere accumulation of knowledge but in the derivation of judgment from experience.

Willisen [1] wisely said regarding experience of war : " It is true war can only be learned by experience ; but

---

[1] Quoted in Count Yorck von Wartenburg's " Napoleon as a General."

what are we to understand by 'experience'?. Who gains experience, the man who has been present during this or that event but has never thought in the least about it, either before or after it, or while it was taking place; or the man who has had no personal experience of such matters but who studies a great number of such wars, and who has always and everywhere examined the causes which produced the results, and learnt from them that certain results always recur if preceded by the same causes, and who has at length formulated views and deduced general principles? Has not the latter 'experience,' and the former none? Shall I not by such experience alone learn to know war, whilst by the other I shall remain altogether ignorant of it?"

Thus we find Napoleon well versed in the art of war before he had any personal experience in the field; and Berthier unable to grasp the very first principles of strategy after twenty campaigns, with the living example of the great Master ever before his eyes.

But study and a knowledge of theory, however complete, are not alone sufficient. The general must also have character, indomitable resolution, iron will, and physical and mental vigour to carry his conceptions to a successful issue; for the ablest plans will not command success unless carried through with resolution.

It is easy to be wise after the event, and the immediate causes of Napoleon's success and of Austrian failure in this initial stage of the campaign are plain. In fact, they rest on the one great principle of war—the application of superior force at the decisive point and moment. Gohier, President of the Directory, said to Napoleon: " You have often beaten the strongest adversary with an inferior force," and received the reply: " The smaller force was invariably overcome by the larger; with inferior forces I like lightning struck the adversary's flank, defeated him there, and then, taking advantage of his disorder, threw myself with all my force upon other points so that on the field of battle I was always stronger than him and beat him in detail."

The fault of the allies lay in the first place in the initial distribution of their forces over so wide a front. In attempting to guard everywhere an extensive line they were weak at all points.

Beaulieu, in his anxiety for the protection of his communications, neglected the maxim of Machiavelli: "Victory annihilates the consequences of the worst operations, and defeat renders useless the best-arranged plans." Or, as Napoleon said: "There is nothing which protects the lines of communication to the rear better than a victorious battle, and for such a victorious battle, which regulates everything and settles every question, one must collect together whatever it is possible to collect."

Beaulieu's next error was in the division of his forces in the attack; not only was Argenteau operating on a line distant from Beaulieu, but separated from him by an impassable obstacle, a great spur of the mountains, and even unable to keep up communication with him. Neither commander could know what was happening to the other, and co-operation was impossible. Beaulieu should have attacked on one line; his forces were insufficient for any other mode of operations.

Had Napoleon really intended to advance by the Bochetta, he would have done well to change his plan on the principle enunciated by Machiavelli: "Immediately change your plans should they become known to the enemy." In any event he chose the best plan, for an attack on the allies' left would, if successful, have merely driven them back on their lines of communication, and led to that concentration of their forces which he desired to prevent. But it was always his habit to aim not merely at victory but at the annihilation of the enemy, and for this purpose he always struck either at their centre or at their strategic flank to drive them off their line of communication.

By good dispositions the initial errors of the allies might still have been to some extent remedied after the defeat of Argenteau at Montenotte, had Beaulieu concentrated the allied forces at some point in the rear, such as Dego. But the Austrians and Piedmontese were acting on divergent lines of communication. Accordingly, as they were defeated in detail and driven back, they became more widely separated, instead of concentrating their forces for resistance at some point in rear, as they might have done had their lines of retreat converged. On this point Napoleon himself said : " The army under the orders of Colli, instead of moving upon Millesimo, should have supported itself on Dego. It was an error to suppose that, in order to cover Turin, Colli must post himself directly upon the road to that city. The armies united at Dego would have covered Milan, because they would have been astride of the high road of Montferrat ; they would have covered Turin, because they would have been near the road to that place. United, the two forces would have been superior to the French army ; separated, they were lost."

The broad, strategical features of this phase of the operations may well be compared with those of the Waterloo campaign, where again Napoleon's plan was to pierce the centre of the widely dispersed allies and defeat them in detail. In that case also the allies were on divergent bases, but by concentrating after retreat instead of retiring on their original lines they were enabled to assemble superior forces on the field of battle, and gain the victory in spite of initial errors.

The position of Serurier's division at the pass of Ormea is noteworthy. He was kept there until the allied centre was broken, in a situation to cover the left of the French advance and to prevent any aggressive action on the part of the Piedmontese. But as soon as the allied centre was pierced, his division was employed in the offensive movement against Colli.

CHAPTER III

Results of the Campaign—New Theatre of Operations—The Passage of the Po—Further Advance—Battle of Lodi—Entry into Milan—Comments

THE terms arranged with Victor Amadeus brought other advantages to the French besides the reduction of the Results of the numbers of their enemies. The Austrians, Campaign deprived of their allies, had now only some 24,000 men in the field, and 12,000 in the fortress of Mantua ; Napoleon had about 32,000 infantry, but his cavalry was inferior to that of his opponent both in numbers and quality.

He had secured a shorter line of communication, which he was careful to guard ; he kept touch with Kellermann's Army of the Alps, while by a special clause the passage of his army over the Po at Valenza was provided for. Before and around him lay the most fertile country on earth, where he could obtain ample provisions. His soldiers would no longer have to fight among the barren rocks of the Apennines, but in a land of plenty, where rich cities would provide them not only with food and clothing, but with arrears of pay long due ; while their enemy was weakened and dispirited, they had a prospect of that glory which was even more dear to the heart of the Frenchman. With a confidence that was in itself a presage of victory, Napoleon wrote to the Directory from Cherasco on the 28th April :

34

" To-morrow I shall march against Beaulieu ; I shall force him to retreat beyond the Po ; I shall cross that river directly after him and seize the whole of Lombardy, and before a month has passed I hope to be on the mountains of the Tyrol."

A glance at the map will show that beyond Pavia and Milan the area of operations was bounded on the north by New Theatre the Alps and Lake Garda, and on the south by of Operations the river Po, to the south of which lay the dukedoms of Parma, Modena, and Bologna, whose neutrality Napoleon was careful to secure.

Beyond the plains of Lombardy, across the Mincio, lay the territory of the Venetian Republic, from which a road led through the Tyrolese Alps into Austria. The plains of Lombardy were crossed by several rivers, the Adda, the Oglio, and the Mincio, falling into the Po. On the banks of the Mincio the great fortress of Mantua stood amid marshy surroundings, and furnished a *point d'appui* for the Austrian army, but, like all fortresses which tend to immobilise armies, constituted as much a source of weakness as of strength.

The first care of Napoleon, whose headquarters were now at Tortona, was to arrange for the passage of the Po. The Passage Beaulieu had assembled his forces between that of the Po river and the Ticino, whence he could guard the crossing from Valenza, where he had been led to expect the French advance. The passage of a river in the face of a well-posted enemy is a difficult matter, as Napoleon was himself to find on more than one occasion during this campaign. But as a river favours to some extent the aggressor, concealing his movements, so it is not always difficult to effect a passage by making a feint at one point and passing it at another.

This was Napoleon's plan. He decided to cross at Piacenza.

Massena, with his division some 8500 strong, was now between Castelazzo and Alessandria. Serurier was at Valenza with orders to make a demonstration as though about to cross the Po at that place. On the evening of the 6th May Napoleon issued orders for the following movements next day :—Massena to Voghera, Laharpe at 5 A.M. to Candelasco, Augereau at 6 A.M. to Castello San Giovanni, Dallemagne at 4 A.M. to Borgo San Antonio.

On the night of the 6th-7th Andreossy and Frontin, with a hundred horsemen, reconnoitred the right bank of the river, and seized some large boats laden with grain and Austrian sick ; at daybreak on the 7th Dallemagne brought to Piacenza 3500 infantry, 1500 cavalry and two guns, and Napoleon superintended the passage of the advanced guard, made in boats at the point of crossing by the Piacenza-Milan road.   At two o'clock in the afternoon the first post under Lannes was established on the far bank of the river, a detachment of 150 Neapolitan horsemen in the enemy's service being driven off by the grenadiers ; the remainder of Dallemagne's force and Laharpe's division followed.   On the same day Joubert made a demonstration of passing the Po at Cervesina ; and the Austrians, expecting the passage to be made about Valenza, where Serurier's division was still standing, turned out and drew up in order of battle on the left bank between that place and San Nazzaro.

Napoleon now directed Massena to march at once for Piacenza, preceding his main body as rapidly as possible with his cavalry and artillery, and on the 9th May his division crossed the Po.   Joubert had also marched for Piacenza on the 7th, and Beaulieu, finding his communications threatened, now hastily abandoned his camp opposite

Valenza, and marched to Casalpusterlengo, with the object of joining Liptay, who was between the Lambro and the Po with 5000 men, and whom he directed to hold Fombio, in order to cover the road to Mantua. But Lannes and Dallemagne drove Liptay back on the 9th, and, leaving a rear-guard at Codogno to cover his retirement, he retreated on Pizzighettone.

Hearing the sound of firing at Codogno, Beaulieu marched on that place on the night of the 9th, and his advanced guard under General Schubirz entered the town which was occupied by Laharpe, who was shot dead by his own men in the darkness and confusion when he turned out on the alarm to join his troops. The Austrians captured some grenadiers, guns and ammunition waggons, but Beaulieu arrived too late to support Schubirz, who was driven out at dawn by Berthier and Dallemagne, and forced to abandon his prizes. Beaulieu retreated to Cremona through Lodi, where he left a rear-guard under Sebottendorf with orders to defend that place, to cover the retreat, and to destroy the bridge if necessary.

On the 9th May also Augereau with his division had crossed the Po by a bridge which he had constructed at
Further Verrua and joined Massena at Casalpuster-
Advance lengo, where Napoleon arrived on the morning of the 10th. The passage of the Po being thus accomplished, it remained to clear Lodi of the enemy in order to open the road to Milan and secure the passage of the Adda. A rear-guard kept the crossing of the Po at Piacenza, and a force was left to watch Pizzighettone, which was garrisoned by a detachment of Liptay's men. Farther back on the line of communication, the reserves of Macquard and Garnier guarded the Apennines and occupied Alessandria and Tortona. A contribution levied at Piacenza replenished the treasury and settled arrears of pay.

Napoleon now directed the march of his troops in three columns, the right column up the bank of the Adda towards Lodi ; the centre by the direct road to Milan, which passed through Codogno and Casalpusterlengo ; the left, from Casalpusterlengo up the valley of the Lambro.

The French columns massed outside Lodi, where Liptay's rear-guard, driven from Codogno, had already given the alarm, and Sebottendorf, who commanded the Austrian rear-guard of 8500 men, was on guard at the bridge with a detachment.

The town of Lodi was built in the form of an amphi-theatre with four bastions, surrounded by ditches, and reached down to the right bank of the Adda.   The few Austrians in the town were driven out by the French skirmishers, and the place was soon in Napoleon's hands The Adda, about one hundred yards in width, was deep and swollen at this season of the year.   Beyond the deep channel of the stream was a small islet, on the farther side of which the water was only some four feet in depth. At this point the bridge from Lodi crossed the river to Revellino on the left bank.

His troops on the hither bank of the Adda having crossed, Sebottendorf caused two spans of the wooden bridge nearest the farther bank to be broken.   It was Napoleon's plan not only to enter Milan, the road to which was now open to him, but to occupy both banks of the Adda, and so be in a position to drive Beaulieu into the Tyrol or Carinthia.   It was necessary to lose no time during which the Austrians could be reinforced on the Adda, and he therefore determined to drive them from the neigh-bourhood of Lodi and from Pizzighettone, farther down the river, and thus secure the approaches to the fortress of Mantua

Napoleon himself reconnoitred the bridge under fire, and had a battery brought up to force the retirement of **Battle of** the Austrian guns which covered the ap- **Lodi, 10th** proaches. From the Madeleine clock tower he **May** was able to survey the Austrian troops across the Adda. Beaumont, who had succeeded Stengel in command of the cavalry, was ordered to cross higher up, at the Mozanica ford, and fall on the enemy's right flank, thus creating a diversion to assist in the passage of the river. In the meantime Massena's guns, which had just arrived, engaged the Austrian batteries for some hours, while Napoleon awaited the effect of Beaumont's action. At length, impatient of delay, he decided to force the passage.

A forlorn hope of volunteers from different corps was to rush the bridge and establish a footing on the other side to cover the passage of the remainder of the army. Led by Massena, Berthier, Dallemagne and Cervoni, the grenadiers, 1000 strong, with fiery tread, fierce shouts and the roll of drums, bearing aloft two standards in their midst, issued from Lodi by the Brescia gate and rushed along the narrow way, six abreast, the brave Dupas in advance. A storm of bullets met the serried ranks; the very bridge shook with the weight of lead, and the groans and clamour of the wounded drowned the fierce cries of the survivors; they shrank appalled, wavered, broke, and gave back before the hell of projectiles. At the entrance to the bridge Massena and Berthier stemmed the waverers with drawn swords. With desperate courage and appeals to the love of glory of their soldiers they led a renewed assault; a party of sharp-shooters, despatched in boats by Napoleon, landed on the islet below the bridge to support the attack, which now pressed forward; on the Lodi bank the bands played martial music, and the fire of the guns, directed by Napoleon, supported the attack. Nothing could arrest the impetuosity of the charge.

Massena and Cervoni leading slid down the broken joists of the bridge that rested on the islet below ; the soldiers followed them ; they plunged into the stream and waded breast high to the farther bank, while the Austrians, appalled, shrank back before the torrent of fierce men who climbed the bank, rushed upon them with the bayonet and dispersed them in all directions, capturing their guns.

It was now seven o'clock in the evening. Sebottendorf evacuated Revellino, the retreat of his infantry being covered by his cavalry, who attacked the French right and did much execution until they were driven back by Kilmaine's squadrons. Beaumont did not arrive in time to take part in the battle, and the Austrians rallied at Fontana, having suffered a loss of 2000 men and 15 guns. From Fontana they made an orderly retreat to Cremona. The French lost about 1000 men.

The road to Milan was now open, and Lombardy was at the mercy of the French. Beaulieu fell back behind the Mincio, while his detachment at Pizzighettone surrendered to the victors of Lodi.

It was while he was at Lodi that the Directory attempted to restrain the ambition and the career of Napoleon. Here it was that in his own mind first arose some conception of his great destiny. Did the French Government also foresee the heights to which their general would rise ? At any rate they feared his ascendancy over the army which idolised him, where the " little corporal " formed the chief subject of conversation over the camp fires, and where his presence at any point was always greeted with acclamations. They proposed to effect a junction of the Army of Italy with the Army of the Alps, for the further conduct of the campaign under the joint command of

Napoleon and Kellermann. But they abandoned the plan on receipt of Napoleon's protest, written at Lodi on the 14th May :

" Kellermann will command the army as well as I, for no one is more convinced than I am that our victories are due to the courage and audacity of the army ; but I believe that to unite Kellermann and myself in Italy is to lose all. I cannot serve willingly with a man who believes himself to be the first general in Europe ; and besides I believe that one bad general is better than two good ones. War is like government, it is an affair of tact."

He would resign his command if the Directory persisted in the proposed course.

The Austrians were followed up for some distance towards Cremona, and the road towards Brescia was reconnoitred and found clear of the enemy, who had retired on Mantua. Pizzighettone, Codogno and Lodi, where the bridge had been repaired, were garrisoned by French troops to secure the line of communication. Massena was recalled to march on Milan, which he entered on the 14th May. Next day Napoleon made his triumphal entry into the chief town of Lombardy amid the acclamations of the populace, who favoured the establishment of a republic. His first act was to demand a contribution of two million livres. The small Austrian garrison refused to surrender and retired to the citadel in the vicinity of the town, which, in the absence of siege guns, could not be immediately reduced.

The 15th May was notable for the conclusion of a treaty between Victor Amadeus and General Clarke, the French plenipotentiary, on behalf of the Directory. This secured Napoleon's line of communication, hitherto uncertain, owing to the possibility of a renewal of hostilities by Piedmont on the termination of the armistice of Cherasco. He was now master of Italy as far as the Mincio.

Napoleon's strategy was bold and effective. He knew what risks to take ; and he took some risk in advancing before the conclusion of a treaty with Victor Amadeus. The armistice of Cherasco might come to an end, and an advance was consequently dangerous, with a possibly hostile Piedmont on his line of communication. On the other hand to stand still was to give the Austrians time to gather fresh strength and resume the offensive in superior force. To advance with a confident army, flushed with success, against a defeated and demoralised enemy was to ensure at least the neutrality of Piedmont. A further victory would clear up everything ; a bold and vigorous offensive would attract the waverers to the side of the Republic, carry with it the initiative, and ensure the maintenance of his army. The rich plains of Lombardy lay before him, an easy conquest.

Comments

The main feature of this phase of the operations was the passage of the Po, which well illustrates in practice Machiavelli's aphorism : " Those enterprises are best which can be concealed from the enemy up to the moment of their fulfilment." Had the passage of the Po been made at Valenza, not only would there have been stubborn resistance to overcome on the part of a prepared enemy ; but Beaulieu when driven back would merely have retired along his line of communication, and might have been able to make a stand again on the Ticino and on the Lambro. As it was, the flank movement to Piacenza secured the country between the Po and the Adda.

It may at first sight be considered that Napoleon's flank march along the right bank of the Po to Piacenza was dangerous, with Beaulieu guarding the Valenza crossing

But the success of the movement was assured by the manner in which it was carried out with secrecy and rapidity, and the flank was protected by the river itself and by Serurier at Valenza. Napoleon's troops were so disposed that up to the last moment he could have concentrated rapidly at any point between Valenza and Piacenza in case of any attempt on his line of communication by the Austrian commander. His march up the right bank of the Adda to Lodi was an operation of a similar nature. The material and moral effect of the victory of Lodi was seen in the submission of Milan, the domination of Lombardy, and the retirement of the Austrians to the line of the Mincio.

Napoleon's own comments on the proposal of the Directory to share his command with Kellermann are sufficient to establish a recognised principle with regard to that point. The proposal was perhaps the outcome of " that idol of superficial minds, the passion for equality." There can be no doubt that an army should be ruled by one brain and not by any council of co-equals such as the Aulic Council of Austria. Concentration is the secret of strength in all things, and unity of command is an essential principle in the conduct of the operations of war. History shows that there is no more fruitful cause of failure than divided counsels and division of authority. In refusing to continue in command of his army in these circumstances Napoleon was undoubtedly right, and his refusal inculcates a principle worthy of imitation, for, as he himself said, " a commander who undertakes to execute a plan which he considers faulty or disastrous is culpable."

CHAPTER IV

THE ADVANCE TO THE ADIGE

Napoleon's Plans—Orders to the Army—Suppression of Revolt—
Theatre of Operations—Austrian Dispositions—Movements
of the French—Passage of the Mincio—Mantua—Political
Affairs—Comments

NAPOLEON'S first care was to reorganise and equip his
army, his weakened battalions being reinforced from the
Napoleon's reserve, while Laharpe's division was distri-
Plans buted among the remainder. But he contem-
plated an early advance with the object of driving the
Austrians out of Italy. Beyond the Mincio they lay in
Venetian territory ; but neither opponent troubled himself about the violation of the neutrality of that ancient
Republic ; a fact not without its significance in relation
to our ideas on the strategic influence of frontiers and
neutral states.

On the 19th May orders were issued for the march of the
Army of Italy, which was to move to the Adda, where
Massena would join the 1st Division, forming the advanced
guard, on the 22nd May. On the 20th Napoleon issued
another of those stirring addresses which electrified his
troops :

" Soldiers ! You plunged like a torrent from the summit
of the Apennines ; you overthrew and dispersed all who
opposed your march. Piedmont, freed from Austrian

tyranny, surrendered to its natural sentiments of peace and amity for France.   Milan is yours; and the Republican flag floats over all Lombardy.   The Dukes of Parma and Modena owe their political exist-ence to your generosity.   The army that menaced you so proudly can no longer oppose a barrier to your courage. The Po, the Ticino, the Adda could not delay you a single day.   Those boasted ramparts of Italy have been of no avail.   You have surmounted them as rapidly as the Apennines.

Address to the Army

" All these successes have filled your country's heart with joy.   Your representatives have appointed a festival dedicated to your victories, to be celebrated in every commune of the Republic.   There your fathers, mothers, wives and sweethearts rejoice in your success.

" Soldiers! you have accomplished much but much remains to be done.   Shall it be said of us that we could conquer but knew not how to reap the fruits of victory ? Shall posterity reproach us with having found Capua in Lombardy ?   But I see you already rush to arms.   You weary of cowardly inaction.   Days lost for glory are lost for happiness.   Let us advance.   We have forced marches to make ; enemies to conquer; laurels to gather ; insults to avenge.   Let those tremble who have whetted the daggers of civil war in France ; who have basely assassin-ated our ministers and burned our vessels at Toulon.   The hour of vengeance has struck !

" But let the people be at ease.   We are the friends of every people, and especially of the descendants of Brutus, of Scipio, and of the great men whom we have taken as examples.   To re-establish the Capitol ; to place there in honour the statues of famous heroes; to awaken the Roman people, torpid through ages of slavery ; these will be the fruits of your victories ; they will mark an epoch in times to come. Yours will be the immortal glory of changing the aspect of the most beautiful part of Europe. The French people, free and respected by the whole world, will give Europe a glorious peace which will repay it for the sacrifices of the past six years. You will return to your homes, and your fellow-citizens will say as they point you out : ' He belonged to the Army of Italy.' "

On the 23rd fresh orders were issued for a further advance, in pursuance of which Massena's division, preceded by the cavalry under Kilmaine, took the Brescia road, which had already been reconnoitred to a considerable distance by Ordener's *chasseurs.*

Serurier covered the right of the advance, and Augereau moved in the centre. Napoleon left Milan on the 23rd **Suppression** May and reached Cremo next day. Here he **of Revolt** heard that an insurrection had broken out in Milan, but did not stop the movement of his army. Having sent orders to the troops in rear to deal with the insurgents, and to shoot the leaders of the movement and all found with arms in their hands, he galloped on to Soncino, to see that all was going on well with the advance, and then turning back reached Milan the same day. A revolt at Pavia was relentlessly suppressed on the 25th, when Napoleon burst into the town, dispersed 8000 peasants who had assembled there, and executed their leaders, while he shot the French commander, who had surrendered. The lives of his soldiers had been spared, and he said that if one Frenchman had been killed he would have razed the town to the ground and erected a column with the inscription : "Here stood Pavia." Swift and sanguinary retributive measures quickly restored order. Napoleon knew how to wage war, for, said he, " war to be effective must be terrible." There were no sentimental cries of " methods of barbarism," in those days. It was understood that neither one's own troops nor the success of military operations should be endangered by any unnecessary tenderness towards enemies.

The new theatre of operations which lay behind the Mincio offered great facilities for defence. The Mincio, Theatre of deep and seldom fordable, flowing from Lake Operations Garda to the Po, was in itself a formidable obstacle. The front to be defended by the Austrians from the strong fortress of Peschiera, at the southern end of Lake Garda, to the great stronghold of Mantua, was only twenty miles in length. In the rear again the alluvial plain, between the gigantic bastions of the Tyrolese Alps and the river Po, was nowhere more than fifty miles in extent, whilst the Adige, another considerable river, offered a second defensive line with a strong place in Verona. And finally, Mantua furnished a last refuge.

At Valeggio, behind the Mincio, Beaulieu assembled 8000 men, including the shattered ranks of Sebottendorf, with Austrian a reserve in rear. Liptay with 5000 was posted Dispositions at Peschiera; Colli was at Goito with 3000 men, and a smaller force guarded the bridge at Borghetto. There were 11,000 in Mantua. The right bank of the Mincio was watched by the Austrian cavalry.

Napoleon's plan was to make a demonstration in the direction of Brescia and Peschiera, to cover the movement Movements towards the real point of attack at Borghetto, of the French where he intended to force the passage of the Mincio. He had his headquarters at Brescia. On the 29th May Kilmaine was with the cavalry at Castiglione. Augereau's division was at Ponte San Marco, on the direct line for Peschiera; Massena, destined to force the passage at Borghetto, was placed far back at Montechiari. Serurier was farther back, at Ghedi. Secrecy was essential to success, and it was not until the 29th May that Napoleon's plans were made known to his generals. Kilmaine was ordered to make a night march with the cavalry and seize the bridge at Borghetto ; he was to be followed immediately by Massena's division, while at the same time Augereau was to advance on Peschiera, Serurier remaining in reserve.

Early on the morning of the 30th May Kilmaine drove the hostile cavalry from the right bank of the Mincio, but **Passage of** was prevented from crossing the bridge by **the Mincio** the fire of the Austrian infantry. But the French infantry coming up, Gardanne, a gallant and skilful soldier, led some carbineers across a ford below the bridge ; and then, covered by the fire of the artillery, the infantry crossed the bridge.   By midday the passage was won, and Beaulieu himself scarcely escaped from Valeggio. Kilmaine, advancing to Castelnuovo, posted his videttes as far as Rivoli on the plain south of Lake Garda. Augereau advanced and occupied Peschiera, the Austrians retiring before him.

Serurier advanced to Guiddizolo ; next day Massena was at Castelnuovo, and on the 1st June his division, accompanied by Napoleon, entered Verona, which he was to hold in order to cover the investment of Mantua by Augereau and Serurier.

Beaulieu, having thrown a force of about 12,000 men into Mantua, retired up the Adige to Roveredo, into the Tyrol.

The Austrians had now been driven out of Italy, where they held only the fortress of Mantua and the citadel at Milan which had not yet surrendered.   Mantua, containing a garrison of 12,000 men, was invested by Napoleon with 7000, with batteries of heavy guns which were collected in the conquered territory ; while Massena, with his headquarters at Verona, pushed his outposts to the slopes of the Tyrolese Alps, and kept a watch on the approaches from Austria. There were roads leading from the Tyrol down both sides of Lake Garda, which were guarded by troops at Salo and Rivoli, the main force being disposed ready to act either on the eastern or western side of the lake in the great plain between Peschiera and Verona. Those places as well as Legnago, lower down the Adige, were fortified.

In the meantime Napoleon was busy establishing order in the conquered country, and in political settlement with Political the various states of Italy, including Venice. Affairs He also turned his attention to Naples, concluding an armistice which detached the Neapolitan cavalry from Beaulieu. He seized the papal legates and levied contributions on the papal states, terrifying the Pope into signing an armistice at Bologna on the 23rd June, under the terms of which the ports of Rome were closed to the enemy, and Bologna, Ferrara, and the city of Ancona were ceded to the French. The Pope had to pay a large indemnity, and many objects of art were delivered up to add to the collection which Napoleon had made with the aid of French savants, for deposit in the museums and galleries of Paris. While pitiless in the suppression of pillage by his soldiers, he filled the coffers of the French Republic with gold and precious stones.

Early in July this political activity was relaxed, partly because all political objects had been attained, and partly by reason of the imminent advance of the Austrians, who hoped to relieve Mantua and regain the ground they had lost. Napoleon, while preoccupied by political affairs, had not neglected the military situation. He saw to his communications, and especially to the security of the passages over the rivers that lay in his rear. He pressed the siege of the citadel of Milan, which surrendered at the end of

D

June, and he gave instructions to Massena, who had 15,000 men, as to the security of the line of the Adige, and the occupation of the approaches from the Tyrol. The fall of the citadel of Milan released a large force to replace Augereau's troops occupied in the siege of Mantua.

The march to the Mincio was a simple operation, and the passage of that river, in view of the scattered situation of the enemy's forces, presented no difficulties. Napoleon had only to present himself in force at the selected point in order to assure the passage. The general movement of his advanced troops in the direction of Brescia masked his real intention of passing at Borghetto with Massena's division, which was held back for the same purpose; his right was protected by Serurier's division echeloned on that flank.

Comments

Beaulieu should have concentrated in a central position, and only watched the river line. As his front was only twenty miles in length, this would not have been difficult. But he made no attempt at concentration at the decisive point. In trying to oppose the French at all points, he was weak everywhere.

Napoleon said later, with regard to the defence of a river line : " The only method is to post one's troops so that they can concentrate in mass, and fall upon the enemy before he has completed the passage."

Once across the Po, Napoleon was able to threaten the Austrian line of communication with the Tyrol and so force Beaulieu to retreat in order to escape being surrounded, as he would have been had he held on at Castelnuovo.

Napoleon's addresses to his troops are worthy of attention. They may sound bombastic to the unimaginative British mind, but they were well calculated to inspire the more lively imaginations of the French, with their love of display, their vanity, and their thirst for military glory They were among the minor factors of success. The most cold-blooded could not but be aroused by such burning words from such a leader.

CHAPTER V

Siege of Mantua—Description of Mantua—Operations at Mantua —Marshal Wurmser—French Dispositions—Austrian Dispositions—Massena driven back—Napoleon concentrates his Forces—Battle of Lonato—Napoleon at Lonato—Battle of Castiglione—Comments

WHILE the Austrians were gathering strength for a fresh advance Napoleon pressed on the siege of Mantua, which **Siege of** for the present formed the principal object **Mantua** of his attention. His headquarters were at Roverbella, where he was conveniently situated in a central position both to watch the lines of the probable Austrian advance and to direct the siege of Mantua. On the 5th July he returned from his operations in Tuscany and the papal states.

Mantua is seated, says the historian Botta, " in the midst of a lake formed by the Mincio in a great depression **Description** above Goito. The lake is divided into three **of Mantua** parts separated from one another by two bridges. The upper bridge, adjoining the Molina gate, where are the mills of the Twelve Apostles, joins the town to the citadel situated to the north. The lower bridge establishes communication between the San Giorgio gate and the faubourg of the same name, situated to the east. The part of the lake towards the embouchure of the river, where it flows into the lake, and the upper gate is called the Superior Lake; the second part between the two bridges, the Middle Lake; finally the third, which extends from the lower bridge to the east of the bridge, has received the name of Inferior Lake. The town is not entirely surrounded by flowing water, because the Mincio, flowing to the left towards the citadel, leaves the right either slightly covered or entirely inundated. That part is overgrown and encloses the marsh which extends round the town from the Pradella gate on the side of Cremona to the Ceresa gate which opens on to the road to Modena.

" Near the Ceresa gate is the castle of T, so-called because its architecture singularly represents that letter. This peninsula, running from the Ceresa gate to the Postierla gate, is joined to the body of the town by several bridges; but its principal issues into the country are by means of the two bridges of the citadel and of San Giorgio, and by the viaducts which lead out across the marsh from the Pradella and Ceresa gates. This marsh, absolutely impracticable, presents a more certain barrier than the lake, which can be crossed by boats. The town had, therefore, to be protected from that side. On the north the citadel was built to defend the entrance from the side of Verona, and to the east the fort of San Giorgio, which defends the place from the side of Porto Legnago.

" The weak part was at the two extremities of the marsh where were the viaducts leading to the principal gates of Pradella and Ceresa. These two viaducts were fortified by means of bastions and various other works.

" Thus, besides the water and the marsh, the greatest strength of Mantua consisted in the citadel, the fort of San Giorgio, the bastions of the Pradella and Ceresa gates, and several others which commanded at intervals the interior of the town, the whole length of its enceinte, and finally the trenches of T and of the Migliaretto.

" Redoubtable by its fortifications, Mantua had also a pestilential atmosphere which, especially in the hot season, spreads infection, disease and death in the neighbourhood. It is especially fatal to foreign armies, unaccustomed to the climate."

Mantua was well supplied with arms and ammunition. Early in June the French had seized the heads of both viaducts, and on his arrival before the place a month later **Operations** Napoleon vigorously pressed the siege. Boats **at Mantua** were armed with guns, batteries were erected, and the trenches, the first of which was begun in Napoleon's presence on the 18th July, pushed towards the enemy's works, which were assailed with shells and red-hot shot. By the end of July the French had closely invested the place and were prepared to carry it by assault, when the attention of the Commander-in-Chief was attracted by more momentous events than the siege of a place which was, after all, but a minor objective ; although, so long as Mantua held out, Napoleon could not carry the war into the enemy's country, but was obliged to stand on the defensive.

Beaulieu had been replaced by Marshal Wurmser, who had 50,000 men under his command. The new Austrian **Marshal** Commander-in-Chief was an Alsatian by birth, **Wurmser** fresh from the field of operations in Germany, but bowed with the weight of over seventy years. He was well known throughout Europe as a brave soldier and able strategist, and he undertook with confidence the delivery of Mantua.

To oppose him Napoleon had some 45,000 men, of whom **French** nearly 10,000 under Serurier were engaged in **Dispositions** the siege of Mantua. Massena had 15,000 at Verona and Rivoli, with a reserve brigade at Peschiera, and Sauret with 4000 holding Salo on the western shore of Lake Garda. Eight thousand were in reserve about Castiglione. Augereau's division was on the Adige at Legnago. In addition some 9000 men were posted in Lombardy and on the lines of communication. Napoleon at Roverbella was in a position to watch the enemy's movements on both sides of Lake Garda. His first care was for his lines of communication, for now, as ever, he left nothing to chance, and however confident he might be of success, he made provision also for failure. On the 24th July he caused inquiries to be made as to the condition of the bridge-heads at Lodi, Piacenza, and Pizzighettone, the principal points on his line through Italy.

Marshal Wurmser's plans were characterised by that fatal obsession which appeared to dominate the Austrians **Austrian** throughout this campaign. He divided his **Dispositions** forces, and not only divided them, but so constructed his plan of campaign that the two portions into which he split his army were separated by the obstacle of Lake Garda. From his headquarters at Trent he despatched Quasdanovich with 18,000 men to march down the western shore of Lake Garda, while he himself with 24,000 moved down the valley of the Adige. A small force also descended the Brenta to advance on Verona by way of Vicenza.

Massena had occupied the fine position of La Corona, north of Rivoli, between Monte Baldo and the Adige, **Massena** where he was attacked by Wurmser on the **driven back** 29th July, and, offering a stout resistance, was forced slowly back by superior numbers; he retired on Roverbella, and eventually on Castiglione, but continued to hold Peschiera with a detachment. At the same time Quasdanovich had driven the French back along the

western shore of Lake Garda, and had taken Brescia, but
Guieu held on to Salo.   Thus driven back on both wings,
Napoleon Napoleon concentrated his forces south of
concentrates Lake Garda, behind the Mincio, his plans being
his Forces facilitated by Wurmser making an unnecessary
march down the Mincio to Mantua.

On this day he wrote to Augereau, thus describing the
general situation :

" The following is the unfortunate position of our army.
The enemy have broken through our line in three places ;
they are masters of La Corona and Rivoli ; two important
points.   Massena has been compelled to yield to superior
forces ; Sauret has evacuated Salo and begun his retreat
to Desenzano, and the enemy has captured Brescia and
the bridge of San Marco.   You see that our communications with Milan and Verona are cut off."

Next day, the 30th July, at Roverbella, whither Augereau had been ordered to retreat, Napoleon gave orders
to his commanders, and issued directions for Serurier to
raise the siege of Mantua, fall back, and take up a position
to cover the line of retreat on Cremona, while reserves were
also called up from the rear.   Serurier, who was on the
point of assaulting Mantua, accordingly destroyed much
of his ammunition, buried his siege guns, and marched
up the Mincio.   Sauret was ordered to march to Salo
again next day, and release Guieu's detachment at that
place.

On the 31st July the Austrian general Ocskay, commanding Quasdanovich's advanced forces, was defeated at
Lonato, where Massena then took up a position.   On the
1st August Augereau retook Brescia, while Quasdanovich
was held at Salo by Guieu.   Next day Wurmser marched

down the Mincio on a useless promenade to Mantua, which he entered in triumph.

On the 3rd August Quasdanovich marched against Massena at Lonato, but was defeated and driven back **Battle of** with heavy loss. Guieu now seized his oppor- **Lonato** tunity, and, issuing from Salo while other French forces co-operated from Brescia and Gavardo, attacked Quasdanovich, who was finally defeated and driven northwards into the mountains, having suffered a total loss of some 3000 men. One wing of Wurmser's divided forces was thus beaten from the field, and Napoleon was in a position to oppose the Austrian Marshal's remaining 25,000 with a superior force of 30,000 men.

On this day a remarkable incident occurred. Two Austrian battalions, cut off from Quasdanovich, marched **Napoleon at** south from Gavardo to Lonato in hope of **Lonato** joining Wurmser, and fell in with and surrendered to Napoleon, who gave the following account of the adventure :—

" During the day I went to Lonato to see what troops could be obtained from there. But what was my surprise, on entering the place, to find the bearer of a flag of truce who summoned the commander of Lonato to surrender, as he was surrounded. Videttes came in with the news that various columns were in touch with our guards, and that the road to Brescia was intercepted at the Ponte San Marco. I saw that these troops must be the remains of the division cut off at Gavardo, which were endeavouring to force their way to the Mincio. This was embarrassing. I had only 1200 men in Lonato. I therefore caused the envoy to be brought into my presence, and his eyes to be uncovered. I told him that if his general had the presumption to capture the Commander-in-Chief of the Army

of Italy, he only had to advance ; that he should be aware
that I was at Lonato, since everyone knew my army was
there ; that all the general officers of his division would be
held responsible for the personal insult offered.   I declared
that if his division did not pile arms within eight minutes,
I would pardon none of them.   The envoy appeared to be
astonished to see me there, and shortly afterwards the
whole column piled arms.   It was 4000 strong, with two
guns and fifty cavalry."

Having relieved Mantua, Wurmser marched up the
Mincio, occupied Borghetto and Valleggio, and laid siege
to Peschiera.   He had hoped to join hands with Quasdanovich at Lonato, but although finding that his lieutenant had been defeated, he still boldly maintained the
offensive and moved towards Castiglione, on a line
extending from Solferino on the right to Medola on
the left.

The French army was on the 5th August in position
covering Castiglione, Massena on the left, Augereau on the
Battle of right, and Kilmaine with the cavalry massed
Castiglione in the rear of the right.   Serurier, coming up
the Oglio after raising the siege of Mantua, was marching
against the Austrian left through Guiddizolo.   Napoleon
made a show of attacking the Austrian right with Massena's
division, until the pressure of Serurier's advance should
make itself felt ; Wurmser extended his right to envelop
the French left, still hoping to join hands with Quasdanovich.

Serurier's division now came up against the Austrian
left and left rear, where Beaumont's cavalry also operated,
and the Austrian advance was thus arrested all along the
line.   The moment for decisive action had arrived ;
Napoleon launched the attack on the Austrian centre,

which had been weakened in reinforcing the flanks and was quickly broken. The French pushed forward to seize the bridge at Borghetto, and then only the brave old Marshal Wurmser, who had drawn his sword and exposed himself in the thickest of the fight, retreated when he found his communications threatened. He was driven beyond the Mincio, which he crossed at Borghetto, and retired towards the Tyrol after suffering a total loss of 15,000 men.

On the 6th August Napoleon was able to write to the Directory : " Thus in five days another campaign has been brought to an end."

On the 7th August Massena occupied Rivoli, and Augereau re-entered Verona. The siege of Mantua was re-established. The Austrians still held the positions of La Corona and Monte Baldo, from which Massena drove them on the 12th August. Guieu, also, was employed in driving back their advanced posts on the western side of Lake Garda, and thus by the middle of August the opposing forces had resumed the situations they had occupied prior to this brief campaign. The Austrian army, which advanced so boldly, had at the end of fifteen days disappeared like a dream.

Napoleon wrote with regard to the Austrian operations :

" Wurmser's plan was defective ; his three corps were separated by two great rivers, several mountain chains, and Lake Garda. He ought to have either debouched with all his forces between Lake Garda and the Adige, or to have advanced with his united army by the Chiesa upon Brescia. In the execution of his plan he made a mistake that cost him dear : he wasted two days in marching to Mantua. He should, on the contrary, have thrown two bridges across the Mincio at

Comments

Peschiera, rapidly crossed this river, joined his right at
Lonato, Desenzano, and Salo, and thus, by quickly uniting
his separated forces, have made good the defects of his
plan."

A besieged place appears to have a curious attraction ;
Wurmser should have remembered that the defeat of the
enemy's army in the field would have automatically relieved
Mantua, and he need not have marched there. We have
seen a similar waste of time and energy in our own day.
Had Wurmser kept in view the principal objective—the
enemy's main army—he might have assailed the French
with superior forces on the 3rd August.

Napoleon has been criticised for not concentrating all
his forces for the siege of Mantua. But it must be remembered that, although he was now on the defensive,
the enemy's main army was still, as always, his principal
objective ; and had he concentrated round Mantua, the
enemy would have been able to cut his communications
with Lombardy and could then have attacked him with
their entire strength, assisted by the garrison of the besieged town. As it was, the investment of Mantua cost
him a great many men from wastage by disease in that
unhealthy spot, and the employment of larger forces would
not have enabled him to reduce the place before the
Austrian advance. He was by every principle of war
right in keeping his army mobile in the field, in preserving
the initiative, and in adopting the offensive, the best
method of defence.

While Wurmser failed to mass his forces on the decisive
point, Napoleon succeeded in doing so, even after his wings
had been driven back on both sides of Lake Garda. His
tactics at the deciding battle of Castiglione were as skilful
as his strategy, and the defeat of the Austrians was ren-

dered certain by the attack of Serurier's division on their weakened flank.

Napoleon's activity during this short campaign was remarkable, but it must be remembered that he was a young man of twenty-seven. During the few days at the end of July and beginning of August he rode five horses to death, and success was largely due to his personal energy and ubiquity. In fact, one of the great lessons of his career and of all history is that of the value of youth. As he himself said, "The grand art of government should be not to allow men to grow old."

Nor is this only a question of physical capacity. Man's life intellectually has been divided into two portions, the ascending and descending, the climax being put at thirty-seven years. It can scarcely be expected that men of advanced years will be able to contend with those in the prime of life, especially in the stress and strain of war. Napoleon, being accused on one occasion of being too young, replied : "Men age fast on the battlefield, and that is where I come from." He also expressed the opinion that "there is little enterprise left in a general after his forty-fifth year."

CHAPTER VI

WURMSER'S LAST CAMPAIGN

Position of opposing Forces — French Advance — Defeat of Davidovich—Movements of Wurmser—Napoleon pursues Wurmser—Fighting outside Mantua—The Austrians driven into Mantua—Comments.

ALTHOUGH they had suffered severe losses and had been driven back beyond the frontiers of Italy, the Austrians **Position of** were still in numbers superior to the French. **the opposing** In the middle of August they were posted be-**Forces** tween the Adige and the Brenta, with their right at Trent, where they received considerable reinforcements.

The French, posted as before from Verona to Peschiera, with advanced posts holding positions beyond Rivoli and Salo, on both sides of Lake Garda, had also been reinforced, and numbered some 42,000 men. But of these Serurier's division, 8000 strong, now commanded by Sahuguet, had resumed the siege of Mantua. Massena was at Rivoli with 14,000 ; Augereau at Verona with 9000. Napoleon had collected a flotilla at Lake Garda, thus establishing communication between his troops on both shores. A fresh division of 11,000 under Vaubois had been formed on the western side of the lake. From his position on the Adige the French Commander-in-Chief could strike at either wing of the Austrian army, too widely separated at Trent and Bassano

Wurmser's plan was to march on Legnago with 25,000 men to raise the siege of Mantua, while Davidovich operated from the Tyrol on the French front with 20,000.

To meet the situation, Napoleon resolved to advance French Advance rapidly up the valley of the Adige, destroy Davidovich's force, and then fall on the Austrians at Bassano and cut them off from the Tyrol.

On the 2nd September Wurmser and Davidovich were far from the front making plans for the destruction of the French. But while their enemies were taking counsel the French army was marching.

On the 1st September orders were issued for Massena and Augereau to move up the valley of the Adige. Vaubois was to march round the northern end of Lake Garda to Torbola. A force of 2000 men under Kilmaine was left at Verona. Should Wurmser march from Bassano to the relief of Mantua, Kilmaine was to retire behind the Mincio, and Sahuguet was in this case to raise the siege of Mantua, and retire behind the Oglio. But Napoleon " thought it unlikely that the enemy would commit this folly."

On the 2nd September Massena's division began the forward movement up the valley of the Adige, and was concentrated at Borghetto, where there was a ford, with the exception of Victor's brigade, which crossed the river by the bridge at Peri. Augereau marched on his right rear to Lugo-Rovere. The Austrian advanced posts under Wukassovich extended south to Ala, beyond which place the road to Trent passed through Roveredo, and farther on at La Pietra through a defile formed by the river on one side and a rocky precipice on the other. This point was commanded by a castle occupied by guns and infantry. It was the key of the Tyrol.

From Trent Napoleon could open communication with Moreau and the Army of the Rhine, with which he might even have joined hands had Moreau marched down the head of the Adige valley.   From Trent also a road ran to Bassano, giving access to the valley of the Brenta, where Wurmser's line of communication might be cut.   In fact, should Wurmser persist in his plan of advancing down the Brenta, the French would debouch in his rear at Bassano, when they had disposed of Davidovich.

On the 3rd September Massena drove back the Austrian advanced posts, and entered Ala, where Napoleon estab-

Defeat of lished his headquarters for the night. Augereau,
Davidovich who had marched from Verona over the hills on Massena's right, advanced on Roveredo next day, while Massena drove Wukassovich out of Marco, and got into touch with Vaubois, who had advanced from Riva and captured Mori.

On the 4th the three columns continued the advance on Roveredo, which was turned by a force under Rampon, who passed along the rocky ground between the town and the Adige, and drove the Austrians out of the castle of La Pietra.   Roveredo was now vigorously attacked, and the Austrians were driven back on Trent, with a loss, in addition to killed and wounded, of 6000 men, who laid down their arms and twenty-five guns.   His force reduced to 10,000 men, Davidovich was obliged to evacuate Trent, which Napoleon entered on the morning of the 5th September.   He at once directed Augereau to occupy Levico, thus securing the road from Trent to Bassano in the valley of the Brenta, while Vaubois followed up Davidovich, pursued him beyond Lavis, and remained in occupation of the road to Innspruck.

In the meantime Wurmser had pursued his plan, and was marching leisurely down the Brenta.   His troops were scattered and on the 6th September he was at Vicenza with his leading division; another division was at Movements Bassano, while Quasdanovich, with the rear of Wurmser division, was at Primolano. Wurmser still thought Davidovich would be able to make a simultaneous advance down the valley of the Adige, and that he himself would raise the siege of Mantua and attack the French south of Lake Garda. His dreams were soon rudely dispelled.

Marching rapidly down the Brenta, Napoleon attacked Quasdanovich at Primolano on the morning of the 7th Napoleon September, and in the pursuit of the Austrians pursues the cavalry captured 2000 men and five guns. Wurmser Following up this advantage, the French general made a long march towards Bassano next day, and, with Massena's division on the right, and Augereau's echeloned on the left, he drove the Austrian rear-guard from the gorges of the Brenta at Cismon. Wurmser now concentrated at Bassano, but Napoleon advanced at two o'clock in the morning of the 8th; the Austrian position was turned; the town and camp were captured; their forces were split up; 5000 prisoners and thirty-five guns were taken. As a result of this battle Quasdanovich was driven to the east towards Treviso, while Wurmser retired in disorder on Vicenza. Napoleon was able to write:

" In six days we have fought two battles and four engagements. We have taken twenty-one standards; we have made sixteen thousand prisoners, including many generals; the remainder have been killed, wounded, or dispersed. In six days, fighting in inexpugnable gorges, we have marched forty-five leagues, captured seventy guns with their waggons, their horses, a portion of their grand park, and magazines.":

E

The Austrian marshal was now in despefate straits, and resolved to take refuge in Mantua. Massena halted Wurmser at Vicenza, while Augereau marched to takes Refuge Padua to cut communications in that direction, at Mantua and prevent a retreat into Friuli; Kilmaine and Sahuguet were instructed to prevent Wurmser from entering Mantua.

Next day, 10th September, Massena crossed the Adige at Ronco, and marched south to cut the Austrians off from Mantua, but General Ott with three battalions turned sharply on his pursuers and drove them back on Ronco with heavy loss. In the six days from 5th to 11th, Napoleon's troops had fought three engagements, and Massena's and Augereau's divisions had both marched over a hundred miles.

In the meantime Augereau had been ordered to march from Padua on Legnago, and arrived before that place, on the opposite bank of the Adige, on the 12th September. Here he was brought to a standstill by a detachment of 1700 men left by Wurmser, which held out until the arrival of Massena on the 13th, when the garrison surrendered. The pursuers being held back by rear-guards, while Sahuguet failed to act, Wurmser was enabled to enter Mantua on the 13th.

The Austrian marshal took up a position outside the place in front of the faubourg of San Giorgio, with an Fighting advanced post in the village of Due-Castelli. outside At daybreak on the 14th Massena advanced Mantua from Castellaro, surprised the Austrians at Due-Castelli, and drove them back upon San Giorgio. Here, however, General Ott turned on the French advanced guard and repulsed them with heavy loss in men and guns. Wurmser renewed the attack, but the French held their ground until the arrival of reinforcements in the evening, when the Austrians were driven back.   In this action there were heavy losses on both sides.

Next morning Napoleon attacked the Austrians with all the forces at his disposal.   Sahuguet, marching down the Roverbellà road, drove them into La Favorita; Augereau attacked their right flank at San Giorgio, while Massena's division, kept for a time in reserve, then fell upon their centre, weakened by reinforcements sent to meet the attacks on either flank.

After severe fighting, in which both sides lost heavily and the French captured twenty-five guns, the Austrians **The Austrians driven into Mantua** were driven into Mantua, where they were closely blockaded.   Kilmaine and Sahuguet were again entrusted with the investment; Massena occupied Verona and the Brenta, and maintained communication with Vaubois in the Tyrol. Augereau formed a reserve in rear.   The total French field army was reduced to a strength of some 24,000 men.

Having disposed of the Austrian aggressive forces for the time being, Napoleon proceeded to Milan, and in **Napoleon's Political and Administrative Measures** October was engaged in settling political affairs with Modena and Rome.   His political activity and acumen were evinced in his dealing with papal intrigues, and in the adroit manner in which he continued to negotiate with the papal court, with which he wished to keep peace for the present.   He had also to settle affairs with Bologna, Medina, Reggio, and Ferrara, while Piedmont, Genoa, and Venice engaged his attention.

His energies were during this time directed to the rogues who robbed and starved his army, but as yet he scarcely had the power to suppress the plundering of the contractors and commissaries, who were engaged in a campaign of peculation, and who battened while his army suffered privations.

This campaign offers a fine example of offensive-defensive warfare. As has already been explained, Napoleon was obliged to act strategically on the defensive so long as Mantua held out. He had not at his disposal sufficient forces to blockade that stronghold, hold Northern Italy, and at the same time invade the enemy's territory. But in adopting the offensive he confused his enemies, upset their plans, and obtained the initiative. His advance up the Adige was a fine stroke of genius, success being obtained by a resolute boldness which was the height of wisdom.

Comments

Rapid movements were the especial feature of this short campaign, and were compared by Jomini to lightning ; but there is nothing new under the sun, for the Chinese strategist Wuntzu had written thousands of years before : " Let your movements be rapid as the lightning ; let your attack be swift as the wind."

It will be observed that Napoleon's columns on this occasion marched to the vicinity of the enemy by different routes ; but the point of junction was carefully fixed at a distance from the Austrian position at Roveredo, so that there was in fact no violation of his principle that " the junction of different columns should never be effected near the enemy." The point of junction was, however, at a place which an active enemy could have occupied before him, and Napoleon himself was not quite satisfied with this movement which, he said, while it was not very dangerous, was not entirely without danger.

The march of Vaubois' column, separated from the remainder by Lake Garda, laid it open to attack ; but Napoleon was well acquainted with the quality of his enemy's strategy

It will be observed how throughout his campaigns he adhered to the principle of operating on one line, and how strongly opposed he was to concentric operations which, carried out with a view to attacking the enemy from more than one direction, expose the various columns to defeat in detail. The disastrous effect of a violation of this principle is seen in the result of the Austrian operations throughout the campaign in Italy. " Separate to live, gather to fight," as Napoleon put it, is still and ever will be a guiding principle of war.

It has been generally held that this principle is in direct conflict with that of Von Moltke, who said : " Incomparably more favourably will things shape themselves if on the day of battle all the forces can be concentrated from different points towards the field of battle itself—in other words, if the operations have been conducted in such a manner that a final short march from different points leads all available forces simultaneously upon the adversary's front and flank." It was in pursuance of such a plan that Serurier marched on the Austrian flank at Castiglione, but the principle was not violated in that case, nor does it conflict with Von Moltke's dictum. Serurier was so situated as to be in easy communication with the French main army. If we analyse Von Moltke's view we shall find that in substance it involves the Napoleonic principle. For, under modern conditions, the various columns march in close communication with each other, even though they may be at considerable intervals, for we have means of communication that were not available in Napoleon's day. They cannot therefore, in the widest sense, be said to be separated from one another, for their movements can be regulated and co-ordinated as though they were marching in one body. We may be sure that Von Moltke himself would not have approved of the

Austrian system, which prevailed in 1796, of forces march-ing to the field of battle, separated from one another by almost impassable obstacles, and in ignorance of each other's movements from day to day.

Under such conditions the march of armies could not be regulated to meet any unforeseen change, such as change in the position of the objective, a very likely contingency where that objective is the hostile army. By keeping forces massed or by keeping them in communication so that their movements can be directed throughout by one master-mind, it is possible to bring them to bear in the mass against the hostile army, even should the latter change its position during the course of the operations preceding actual contact.

CHAPTER VII

THE BATTLE OF ARCOLA

State of the French Army—Situation of the Austrians—Alvinzy
—Austrian Plans—Movements of Davidovich—The French
retire — Austrian Position — Situation of Napoleon — He
attacks Alvinzy—Is driven back on Verona—Napoleon's
Resolution—The Movement to Ronco—Arcola—Battle of
Arcola, 15th November—16th November—17th November
—Defeat of Alvinzy—Davidovich driven back—Politics and
Administration—Comments

THE fierce fighting of September, the pestiferous camp
around Mantua, and the necessity of blockading that place
State of the with its large garrison had greatly reduced the
French French army, and left Napoleon with a field
Army force of only some 24,000 men. He continued
to demand reinforcements from the Directory, but received
only five or six thousand men. He knew well his own
weakness, but assumed a bold front to enemies and friends
alike, threatening the Austrian Emperor with the destruction of his position on the Adriatic unless he made
peace, while to his army he showed a confidence which he
must have been far from feeling, but which formed a
considerable factor of success.

Napoleon reached Verona on the 23rd October. He had
timely information that the Austrians were gathering
Situation of strength both in the Tyrol and on the Piave,
the Austrians with a view to making a fresh effort to retrieve
their fortunes. On the Rhine the Archduke Charles

had met with some successes, and pushed back Moreau and Jourdan across that river, thus enabling the Austrian Emperor to transfer a portion of his forces to the Italian theatre of operations. By the end of October 28,000 Austrian troops were assembled on the Piave and Tagliamento, while Davidovich's army in the Tyrol, at the head-waters of the Adige, was increased to 20,000 men.

The supreme command was entrusted to Alvinzy, an officer of the old school, brave and obstinate, who had **Alvinzy** gained distinction in the Turkish wars. He was, however, too old, being over sixty years of age. As this campaign proved, and as all history teaches us, the younger commanders gained the greatest successes, and the old Austrian leaders were venerable creatures of routine, like those Prussian generals who shared in the debacle of Jena ten years later.

Alvinzy's Chief of the Staff, Weyrother, was reputed to be a scientific officer, but possessed a mind that worked in a narrow groove, and was unable to judge of the application of principles according to circumstances, and to analyse cause and effect. He failed in this campaign as he failed nine years later at Austerlitz, notwithstanding that he had at his disposal the experience of past Austrian disasters and French successes.

Alvinzy and the Chief of the Staff resolved to operate on two lines. From his headquarters in Friuli the Austrian **Austrian** marshal would cross the Piave and the Brenta, **Plans** and march on Verona with 28,000 men ; while Davidovich at the head of 20,000 advanced from Botzen down the valley of the Adige. Verona was chosen as the point of concentration of the two armies, from whence they could drive the French across the Mincio and relieve Mantua, from which Wurmser also could perhaps issue and co-operate.

Napoleon took no immediate action, but awaited the development of circumstances which would furnish a guide for a plan of operations. His troops were posted as before. Vaubois was in the Tyrol, with headquarters at Trent; Massena was at Bassano; and Augereau at Verona.

On the 30th October Alvinzy massed his troops behind the Piave, which he crossed on the 1st November. Massena, **Advance of** who had remained in observation on that river, **Alvinzy** withdrew his advanced posts to Bassano, and on the 4th retired from that exposed position to Vicenza, and from thence to Montebello, to which place Augereau had been advanced by Napoleon.

In the meantime Davidovich had marched in force down the Adige from Botzen. Vaubois attacked him at Lavis **Movements** on the 2nd November, but the Austrians, **of Davidovich** strongly reinforced, advanced next morning and drove the French out of Trent and through Roveredo, Further fighting took place on the 6th and 7th November, when Vaubois was driven back from the defile of Caliano, and forced to retire to Rivoli, having suffered a loss of 3000 men and six guns.

Napoleon directed Massena to advance on November 6th and attack the Austrians about Citadella, behind the **The French** Brenta, where they had taken up a position. **retire** Here Liptay, supported by Provera, made a desperate stand, and a bloody and prolonged combat ensued, which ended in Massena retiring beaten to Vago and San Martino, in front of Verona. Augereau, who was co-operating, after a preliminary success against the Austrian advanced posts at Bassano, was repulsed at the same time. Both Massena and Augereau were withdrawn to Verona. Alvinzy entered Vicenza on the 8th and Montebello on the 9th November.

On the 11th he occupied a strong position from Colognola to Caldiero, covering the road from Vicenza to Verona **Austrian** with his reserve in Villanova. The strength **Position** of his position lay in the heights of Caldiero, at the foot of the Tyrolese Alps, of which Jomini says : " The heights of Caldiero are the spurs of the mountains of Sette Communi, which slope gradually to the Adige, and cross the post road from Verona to Vicenza. These heights, steep and covered with vineyards, guarded on one side by the river and on the other by the lofty mountains from which they spring, form one of the most remarkable of military positions."

Napoleon had now concentrated 21,000 men about Verona, while holding Rivoli and La Corona with Vaubois' **Situation of** division of 8000, disposed by Massena, who had **Napoleon** been sent there for that purpose, for the defence of the position between the Adige and Lake Garda; he had a garrison in Legnago. Sahuguet with 8000 men was still blockading Mantua. The situation appeared sufficiently desperate, and a commander less enterprising than Napoleon would probably have retired at least to the line of the Mincio. Should Alvinzy and Davidovich succeed in uniting, the Austrian forces would be overwhelming. But " he who wishes to make quite sure of everything in war, and never ventures, will always be at a disadvantage ; boldness is the acme of wisdom." The French Commander-in-Chief decided on a bold course. He would make a counter-attack on Alvinzy's army at Caldiero.

On the 12th Napoleon attacked the Austrian position, Massena assailing their right while Augereau moved against **He attacks** the left. Both divisions at first met with some **Alvinzy** success. Massena drove back the enemy from their posts on the heights of Colognola ; but his soldiers met with a snowstorm driving in their faces at the moment when the Austrian right was largely reinforced by the brigades of Schubirz and Provera, and he was driven back with a loss of nearly two thousand men and two guns. Is driven   Augereau, who had advanced against the back on   enemy's front at Caldiero, was forced to con- Verona   form to the retirement on Verona.   Next day Alvinzy advanced to Vago, and his cavalry even appeared before Verona.   At the same time Davidovich was slowly pushing back Vaubois, and the situation seemed blacker than ever.   While sustaining the courage of his soldiers and making a show of confidence, Napoleon wrote to the Directory on the 18th November :

" All our superior officers, all our best generals are *hors de combat*.   The Army of Italy, reduced to a handful of men, is exhausted.   The heroes of Millesimo, of Lodi, of Castiglione and of Bassano have died for their country or are in hospital.   The corps have remaining only their reputation and their pride.   Joubert, Lannes, Lanusse, Victor, Murat, Chabot, Dupuy, Rampon, Chabran, Pijon, Saint Hilaire, Menard, are wounded.   We are abandoned in the interior of Italy.   The brave men remaining regard death as inevitable amid chances so continual and with forces so inferior in numbers.   Perhaps the hour of the brave Augereau, of the intrepid Massena, of my own death is at hand."

But his resolution was unshaken, and his genius for war never gleamed more brightly than when the masses of his Napoleon's enemies appeared like dark and threatening Resolution   clouds on the horizon, lit up by the flash of arms and accompanied by the rumbling thunder of distant drums.   It has been well said that only the man who is constantly occupied with great thoughts will be able to form a great resolve when the decisive moment appears.

The 13th and 14th November were uneventful. Napoleon occupied himself in preparing his troops for the coming struggle, in seeing to their equipment and replenishing their ammunition. Alvinzy awaited at Caldiero the approach of Davidovich, whose advance was slow but who steadily pushed back the French troops opposed to him. Napoleon was forming a great resolve. He would leave a portion of Vaubois' division to hold Verona, march down the Adige to Ronco, construct a bridge and cross the river there, and attack the Austrian flank at Arcola, which stands on the left bank of the Alpon, a tributary of the Adige, a short distance above its junction with that river.

Ronco, eleven miles down the Adige from Verona, offered a good position for defence and several roads by which The Move- the Austrians could be assailed. A short ment to distance below Ronco, the deep river Alpon, Ronco flowing between high banks, joins the Adige near Albaredo, forming between the two streams a tract of marshy ground crossed by causeways connecting the neighbouring villages. One of these roads, raised above the level of the surrounding country, leads across the marsh from Ronco on the Adige to Arcola on the Alpon. Another similar road ran from Ronco to Porcil and Caldiero. From Villanova and Arcola was a road leading to Albaredo and Legnago.

The small village of Arcola stood about a hundred and fifty yards from the left bank of the Alpon, which was Arcola there crossed by a wooden bridge; but close to the bridge were a few low houses, from which the way could be defended, and a square tower protected the approach. The country generally was well

crossed the Adige in boats at Albaredo; they took that place, and at seven o'clock in the evening a force under Guieu attacked the Austrians at Arcola and drove them out of the village with heavy loss. But the French had to evacuate the place a few hours later, failing support from Augereau's division, driven back as already related, and fearing that the enemy might surround them. It was reoccupied by the Austrians at daybreak on the 16th November.

On this morning Augereau and Guieu again passed the Adige, but they were driven back by superior forces, and again obliged to retire on Ronco. Later, 16th November Colonel Vial found a ford, but the soldiers refused to follow their officers. Massena's division met with some success. They advanced along the road to Porcil, drove back the Austrians, taking 1600 prisoners and seven guns and bivouacked before that place.

On the 17th November a French detachment from Legnago marched up the left bank of the Adige to make a demonstration against the Austrian left, and 17th November were joined at Albaredo by Augereau's troops, which captured that place. The combined force then marched against Arcola, but the Austrians on the right bank of the Alpon now drove back the French, who were in front of them, on Ronco, and the force on the left bank thereupon gave up their enterprise, and retreated again on Albaredo. The French right was now driven back on the bridge at Ronco, but the Austrian pursuing column was in turn assailed on both flanks by Massena from the Porcil direction and by a force concealed behind the Ronco-Arcola causeway, and was almost entirely captured or destroyed.

Augereau once more advanced, but was unable to force the passage to Arcola until a number of trumpeters, under

Lieutenant Hercule, despatched by Napoleon across the river, sounded the charge in the Austrian rear. Panic-stricken the Austrians rapidly retreated ; Augereau ad-**Defeat of** vanced upon Arcola, and Massena at the same **Alvinzy** time, having driven back the Austrian right on Caldiero, marched also on Arcola. The battle was at an end. Alvinzy retired on Montebello, leaving the field of action to the French. Ths Austrians lost in the three days' battle some 6000 men and eleven guns ; while the French casualties numbered 4500. Napoleon himself wrote to Carnot, Minister of War : " Never has a battlefield been more strenuously disputed than that of Arcola."

While the battle of Arcola was in progress, Joubert, who had taken command of Vaubois' division, was attempting **Davidovich** to hold back Davidovich, who advanced against **driven back** the French position at Rivoli on the 17th November. Advancing in superior force down the Adige, the Austrians attacked and drove back the French posts on the Monte Baldo, and forced Joubert to retire to Peschiera. But Davidovich had begun his advance too late. The battle of Arcola was over. Massena and Augereau were ordered up to support Joubert, and Davido-vich was driven back on Roveredo. Alvinzy, relieved by these operations from the pressure of pursuit, had again moved to Caldiero, but when Davidovich was forced to retire, he once more retreated and took up a position behind the Brenta.

Wurmser was to have co-operated with the Austrian advance, but he did not make his sortie until Alvinzy had already been defeated, and, the blockading force having been reinforced, he was driven back into the citadel when he attempted to break out at San Giorgio.

The remainder of the year 1796 was occupied by

Napoleon with political affairs, and with the organisation
Politics and   and equipment of his army.   He was engaged
Administra-   in negotiations with the Vatican, and in the
tion   settlement of Modena and Lombardy, regarding which he wrote to the Directory on the 28th December :

" There are three parties in Lombardy ; first, those who
are led by the French ; second, those who desire liberty ;
third, the friends of the Austrians and enemies of the
French. I sustain and encourage the first, control the
second, and repress the third."

From his headquarters at Milan he renewed his campaign
against the peculation and corruption that were rife in the
civil departments of the army, regarding which he wrote :

" The keepers of magazines forge orders, and share with
the commissaries ; luxury, depravity, and peculation exist
in the highest degree."

Against these people he waged relentless war, receiving
but little support from his Government.   He called in vain
for 30,000 men to reinforce his wasted army ; only a few
thousands were sent to him early in 1797.

In this phase of the campaign we see Napoleon still on the
defensive, saving himself from a perilous situation only
Comments   by the exercise of great courage and resolution.
              These qualities alone, a determination not to
be beaten, and an invincible persistence, enabled him to
wear down the enemy and snatch a victory almost from
the ashes of defeat.   These operations exemplify the
advantage of offensive tactics, even with a force numeri-
cally inferior, and operating on the defensive.

The Austrian operations again proved the danger of

F

neglecting the fundamental principle that the junction of columns moving independently should not be arranged for at a point in occupation of the enemy, already fully dealt with in the preceding chapter. From beginning to end the Austrian operations exhibited a want of concentration of effort and of force at the decisive point. The various Austrian forces, including those at Mantua, acted in a desultory manner and with an absence of that continuous energy which was necessary to success. Instead of attacking simultaneously they acted independently of one another, and so were beaten in detail

CHAPTER VIII

THE BATTLE OF RIVOLI

Situation in December 1796—Austrian Plans—French Dispositions —Situation, 12th January 1797—Joubert at Rivoli—Battle of Rivoli—Massena's Arrival—Defeat of Alvinzy—Provera marches to Mantua—Capture of Provera's Force—Surrender of Mantua—Napoleon at Rome—Comments

AFTER the battle of Arcola, Massena occupied Verona, Augereau taking up an advanced position on the road to **Situation,** Vicenza, while Joubert with 10,000 men occu-**December** pied La Corona and Rivoli. Serurier had **1796** resumed command of the troops blockading Mantua, the garrison of which, as Napoleon learnt from an intercepted despatch, was now in sore straits. But the Austrian Emperor determined once more to tempt the fortunes of war, encouraged no doubt by the disturbed political state of Italy and by successes on the Rhine. The army under Alvinzy was strongly reinforced, and every effort was made to prepare for the coming struggle. The Austrian general had 42,000 men under his command, on a line extending from Padua through Bassano to Roveredo and Ala.

Alvinzy and his Chief of Staff, Weyrother, formed a plan of attack in three columns. Provera was to march from **Austrian** Padua on Legnago with 8000 men, and thence **Plans** to the relief of Mantua, the garrison of which was expected to co-operate with him ; 6000 under Bajalich would assail Verona ; Alvinzy himself with 28,000 would advance down the valley of the Adige, and approach Verona from the north, marching in several columns by different routes upon Rivoli in the first instance. Their main lines of advance were separated by mountains and rivers.

To meet this attack Napoleon had some 30,000 men, exclusive of 14,000 under Serurier blockading Mantua. **French** An intercepted despatch had given him timely **Dispositions** information of the enemy's projects, but he awaited their development before adopting any plan to meet them. With his troops in a central position guarding Verona and the line of the Adige, on which Augereau had his main body at Ronco and a strong post at Legnago, while Rey commanded a reserve in a central position behind the Mincio, he was ready for all eventualities.

Napoleon reached Verona on the 12th January 1797, and took a rapid survey of the situation. Bajalich had **Situation,** halted on the Vicenza road, after being driven **12th January** back from San Michele with a loss of 1500 **1797** men; Provera was holding back before Legnago. Joubert, posted on La Corona, had enemies closing in on every side—Lusignan on the Monte Baldo on his left; Liptay with 12,000 assailing his front; while Quasdanovich and Wukassovich were descending the Adige and approaching his right.

Joubert, pressed by the oncoming hostile columns, fell back on Rivoli; and Napoleon, now certain that this was **Joubert at** the enemy's main attack, hastened thither, **Rivoli** ordered up reinforcements from the other divisions, and directed Rey to advance to Castelnuovo, where he would get orders for his march to the battle-field.

On the night of the 13th Massena marched to Rivoli with a large portion of his division, and in the early morning

debouched into the Rivoli plain and found himself in the
presence of the enemy.

Napoleon had during the night proceeded to Rivoli,
visited the outposts, encouraged the soldiers by his presence
and his promise of victory, and reconnoitred from a distance the Austrian camps. The night was bitterly cold, and
snow lay thick upon the ground ; but in the bright moon-
light the position of the Austrians could be clearly distinguished.

The plateau of Rivoli is formed by the mountains which
descend to the right bank of the Adige and Lake Garda.
From the north, along the bank of the Adige, a road leads
to Rivoli, passing through the village of Incanale and
across the heights of San Marco, crowned by a chapel
which was one of the most contested posts on the day of
the battle. The plateau is thus shut in by San Marco,
La Corona and Monte Baldo on the east, north, and west.
On the left bank of the Adige another road runs parallel.
At Rivoli all the paths over the mountains meet, except
one across the Monte Baldo, which forms the northern
buttress of the plateau, passing some distance to the west.

The morning of Saturday the 14th January 1797 found
Alvinzy with some 25,000 men engaging Joubert's 10,000.

Battle of The Austrian general had united three columns
Rivoli between Caprino on the right and the chapel of
San Marco on the left ; Lusignan's column was advancing
to the north of Monte Baldo ; and the troops of Quasdanovich and Wukassovich were pouring down the roads on
either side of the Adige. There was not, however, that
close co-operation between them which is necessary in concentrating troops from different points towards the field of
battle ; and they were separated from one another by
serious obstacles, by precipitous heights, and by a considerable river

Before daybreak the French were moving on the road from Rivoli to Incanale, and Joubert attacked and drove the Austrians from the chapel of San Marco, which was taken by Vial's brigade, while the Austrian centre was also driven back and their right was vigorously assailed. But French reinforcements had not yet arrived, and Joubert's small force could make but little head against the overwhelming numbers of their enemies, who made counter-attacks at all points. A fierce fight, with varying fortunes, took place about San Giovanni on the French left, where Liptay, arrived before Caprino, attacked in force. But at this time, at nine o'clock in the morning, Massena's **Massena's** troops arrived on the field of battle. At some **Arrival** points the French were holding their own, but Vial had been driven from the chapel of San Marco by superior forces, the Austrians being constantly reinforced. Neither Lusignan nor Wukassovich had, however, reached the scene of action when Massena's troops debouched on to the plateau of Rivoli on Joubert's left.

Massena's guns reinforced those of Joubert, which were in battery before Camporengo, behind which place the French cavalry were massed, and brought a devastating fire to bear on the Austrian columns. This stopped their advance at ten o'clock, when they took cover to the left of San Marco. Massena's infantry was now massed near the village of Rivoli : Napoleon was with them. At half-past ten Massena led his troops on Trombalora, on the French left, while Napoleon, posted on an eminence, watched their advance and animated them with voice and gesture.

Advancing over difficult ground, through snow and in face of a storm of bullets, the French grenadiers pressed on, attacked their enemies with the bayonet, and drove them back, though in good order, from the heights of

Rivoli, so fiercely contested and so honourable to both armies, the Austrians lost 3400 killed and wounded, 7000 prisoners and five guns ; the French casualties numbered 2200 men.

While this battle was in progress, Bajalich from Vicenza demonstrated against Verona to cover Provera, who had

Provera marches to Mantua

marched to the relief of Mantua. On the 13th January Provera threw a bridge across the Adige at Angiari, thus evading Augereau, who was at Legnago, and marched to attack Serurier at Mantua. Napoleon heard of this movement on the night of the battle of Rivoli. Ordering Massena to follow with a portion of his division, he set out for the new scene of action. Augereau had in the meantime followed Provera, and attacked and severely handled his rear-guard.

Massena marched on the morning of the 15th January, and after a short halt at Roverbella arrived before La Favorita in the evening. At midnight the garrison under Marshal Wurmser made a sortie in the hope of joining Provera, but were driven back by Massena's troops.

Capture of Provera's Force

Provera had already attacked San Giorgio, but had been repulsed. Next day, after a desperate resistance, finding himself surrounded, the Austrian general surrendered with his 7000 men and 30 guns.

Wurmser, deprived of all hope of aid, was still closely blockaded in Mantua. He had seen the army sent to succour him perish or surrender to a man ; 18,000 Austrians and 6000 of the inhabitants had been killed or had died during the siege ; the survivors were reduced to the last extremity and forced to devour cats and dogs in order to sustain life, which at the best of times was precarious in that pestiferous spot, where the besiegers had themselves lost some 7000 men.

On the 3rd February 1797 the gallant old soldier who, Napoleon wrote, had " never ceased to show courage and **Surrender of** constancy," surrendered with his garrison of **Mantua**   16,000 men, all that remained of an army of 30,000. The troops marched out with the honours of war, and laid down their arms. Wurmser with his Staff and an escort were allowed to go free. The remainder were sent to Austria after undertaking not to serve against the French for a year; 1500 guns were found in the place.

After the fall of Mantua, Napoleon proceeded with 8000 men to Rome, determined to come to a settlement **Napoleon at** with the Papal States, which had shown covert **Rome**   hostility so long as the campaign had proceeded with uncertainty as to the fate of Italy. But with the fall of Mantua the Austrians were finally driven from Italian soil, and on the 18th February the Pope agreed to terms dictated by Napoleon in a treaty signed at Tolentino.

The repetition of Austrian errors is as wearisome as it is incomprehensible, depending in these operations, as **Comments**   throughout the whole campaign, on the neglect of the same primary principle of war—the concentration of strength and of effort for the attainment of the main object, the destruction of the hostile forces in the field.

At Rivoli Napoleon proved himself no less a master of tactics on the field of battle than of strategy on the theatre of war. A scientific artillery officer, he showed what could be done by a judicious employment of guns, regarding which we have his own saying that " great battles are won with artillery."

His restless activity and the energy with which he inspired his troops are evinced in his march to Mantua from the battlefield of Rivoli, exemplifying his dictum that " nothing is done so long as anything remains to be done." Now, as after Austerlitz, he considered victory incomplete as long as any of the enemy's forces remained in the field. His activity of mind and body, and his dauntless resolution are to be seen in the manner in which he undertook and carried to a successful issue the operations in which he contended in succession with four Austrian armies, maintaining throughout the freshness and vigour of his brain. Such stress and strain of war would have worn out a lesser spirit.

In this as in his subsequent campaigns we find the same characteristics : separating to live ; gathering to fight ; the rapid concentration on the decisive point ; the lightning blow ; the relentless pursuit, following on dispositions made not merely with a view to defeat, but to destroy the enemy. The operations of the campaign in Italy foreshadowed those to be carried out on a greater field of action and with great masses of troops, when victory would mean not merely a set-back to the enemy, but the fall of dynasties and the fate of empires.

The holding of Mantua affords one more illustration of the influence of a fortress on the fortunes not only of its garrison but of their field army, which it tends to immobilise. The fortress is liable to assume in the eyes of those who would relieve it an undue importance, and its relief may become the main objective to the exclusion of the proper objective, which cannot be too frequently insisted upon, the enemy's army in the field. The defeat of the enemy in the field entails automatically the relief of the fortress, and their main army and that alone, and not any geographical place or spot, constitutes the decisive point.

Mantua was no doubt of great importance in this campaign ; so long as the Austrians held it, Napoleon could not advance beyond the frontiers of Italy, and was kept on the defensive when he reached the line of the Mincio and Lake Garda. The losses on both sides, due to its climate, serve to illustrate Napoleon's maxim : " It is better to fight the most sanguinary battle than to encamp troops in an unhealthy locality."

CHAPTER IX

THE INVASION OF GERMANY

The Archduke Charles—Napoleon's Situation—His Plans—Preliminary Movements of the French—The Theatre of Operations—Massena's Advance—Austrian Position—Instructions for Joubert—Passage of the Tagliamento—The Archduke retreats—Massena reaches Tarvis—Flight of the Austrians—Napoleon on the Summit of the Alps—Final Stand of the Austrians—End of the War—Comments.

ALTHOUGH so frequently and signally defeated, the Austrians decided to undertake one more campaign. The Arch- For this purpose, and to defend their own duke Charles frontier, the remains of Alvinzy's army, reinforced by troops withdrawn from the Rhine, were placed under command of the Archduke Charles, one of the ablest soldiers in Europe, who was afterwards destined to oppose Napoleon on the banks of the Danube. In contrast to the veteran Austrian generals who had hitherto been employed, the new Commander-in-Chief was even younger than his great opponent, being only twenty-five years of age. The Archduke had, early in March, some 40,000 men in Friuli and the Tyrol.

Napoleon had been strongly reinforced. A return, dated the 10th March 1797, shows that he had under his command Napoleon's close upon 60,000 men, of whom nearly 43,000 Situation formed the active force in the field, the remainder being in reserve and on the line of communication. He began the campaign with greater advantages in point of numbers and *moral* than he had hitherto possessed.

93

Mantua, having fallen, no longer necessitated the detachment of a large force, and the obligation of standing on the
defensive. Continual success had raised the ardour and
prestige of his troops, and correspondingly diminished those
qualities in their opponents. He could carry the war into
the enemy's country. He had the advantage of the
initiative which he hastened to adopt, his enemies standing
on the defensive and awaiting reinforcements which could
nor reach them until April. But Napoleon had a long
line of communication to guard, and the fact that he had
in his rear enemies active and potential caused him to cast
many an anxious glance behind him before leaving the
plains of Italy to march into Germany.

After due consideration Napoleon adopted the bold
course of attacking the enemy and invading their territory.
His Plans Delay would admit of reinforcements reaching
the Austrian army ; he resolved on an early
resumption of the campaign. He decided to advance
broadly on two lines. His main army would move through
Venetian territory and force the passage of Tagliamento,
behind which the Archduke Charles was assembling his
forces. At the same time Joubert, operating through the
Tyrol, would move towards Carinthia, and the two forces
would unite in the valley of the Drave, the main army
having advanced north-east across the Carnic Alps. The
French army would them be in a position to march on
Vienna.

The main French army, its divisions under command of
Preliminary Massena, Guieu, Bernadotte,[1] and Serurier,
Movements advanced on a broad front, and crossed the
of the French Brenta between Padua and Bassano at the end
of February. From Bassano, Massena moved a force up

---

[1] Bernadotte had been with the Army of the Rhine, and only joined
his division at Bassano.

the valley of the Brenta, the Austrians offering resistance to the passage at Carpene, where they were defeated with loss on the 26th February. Primolano was occupied by the French on the 1st March ; at this point a road enters the Tyrol by way of Levico to Trent, and communication was here established with Joubert. Feltre was occupied without resistance. The other division, on Massena's right, had meanwhile advanced across the Brenta and approached the Piave.

The theatre of operations that lay before the French army offered a strong contrast with that in which they had **The Theatre** been engaged in the plains of Italy. Before **of Operations** them rose the rocky, precipitous, and snow-clad summits of the Alps, from which the head-waters of the Piave, the Tagliamento, the Isonzo, the Drave and their tributaries poured through dark and gloomy ravines, where the narrow roads appeared as though they might easily be defended by a few resolute men.

From Verona two roads led into Austria : one through the Tyrol to Innspruck by way of Trent and Brixen ; the other through Vicenza and Udine, which, passing Gemona and over the heights of Tarvis, crossed the Carnic Alps and descended to Villach on the Drave. Beyond the Tagliamento a road through Udine and Laybach turned northward to join this route at Tarvis, after traversing the valley of the Save. The season was yet early, and a halt was made until the 9th March, for the passes of the Alps were closed still by snow.

On the 10th March Massena's main body quitted Bassano ; his advanced troops had pushed on, as already related, **Massena's** to Feltre. On reaching Belluno the French **Advance** general found an Austrian force under Lusignan in occupation of that place. Massena drove him out with Rampon's brigade, pursued him, and captured him and

600 of his men after a fight at Polpet on the 13th. The remainder of Lusignan's force dispersed. On that date the whole of the French army was across the Piave.

Massena, having cleared his front of enemies, now turned to his right towards Aviano. Napoleon had been awaiting his appearance, and had massed his remaining divisions ready to force the passage of the Tagliamento as soon as his left should be thus secured.

The Archduke Charles had assembled his main forces on the Tagliamento, between Spilimbergo and San Vito.
Austrian   Napoleon's plan was to cross the river, force
Position   the Austrians back, and advance on Vienna by
way of Gemona, Villach, Klagenfurth, and the Semmering Pass. Massena was already established on this route, and Joubert would join in from the Tyrol at Villach.

On the 15th March Napoleon issued, from his head-quarters at Sacile, the following instructions to Joubert,
Instructions explaining his plans and showing that, although
for Joubert   bold and confident, he had provided for all
eventualities. He had already written to Massena from Conegliano, predicting the decisive success towards which events were tending.

" In order to form a junction of the forces in the Tyrol with those in Friuli, the latter must cross the Tagliamento, seize the position at Osoppo, force the passes of Pontebba, and reach the valley of the Drave.

" The divisions from the Tyrol should enter Brixen and drive the enemy beyond the mountain range between Innspruck and Brixen. But military contingencies require that possible events should be provided for in advance.

" First : The division from the Tyrol may be defeated and obliged to fall back upon the line of Mori, or even that of Rivoli ; be driven into the intrenched camp of Castelnuovo, and reduced to defend the Mincio, or even obliged to take refuge in Mantua.

" Second : The enemy may endeavour to penetrate by Feltre and Primolano, in attempting to cut our communications ; this, in present circumstances, appears to me very difficult.

" Third : It may be that by one or other movement the divisions in Friuli will be outflanked on the right or left, and that a hostile column may thus reach the Piave, and even the Brenta, before the Friuli divisions.

" Should the first hypothesis prove correct, but only in this case, you will act on the order which I send, giving you command of the division in the district of Mantua as well as in Lombardy, and the whole of the country between the Oglio and the Adige.

" In every case you must provision and hold Peschiera, Porto Legnago, Mantua and Pizzighettone ; post yourself between Mantua and the Po, in a position to supply yourself by that river and to fall on the enemy's rear if he should advance into the Milanese ; inform General Sahuguet that he is to concentrate his forces at the castle of Ferrara. I shall give you, moreover, as much freedom as exigencies demand, assured that in all circumstances you will act in accordance with the spirit of the war in which we are now engaged.

" If you are beaten, you understand that it is essential to dispute every position, and to employ all your resources and those of the natural features of the ground in order to give the Friuli divisions time to take appropriate measures.

" You will find enclosed detailed instructions in the different eventualities which may arise.

" Prepare to attack Botzen from the most convenient direction, taking the snows into consideration.

" To-morrow we shall make the passage of the Taglia-

G

mento, which it is said the enemy intends to dispute. I
wish you to begin your movement on the 27th or 28th. If
the weather continues fine as it is now, and fortune favours
us, I expect to be in the defiles of Pontebba on the 30th ;
that is, on the road from Udine to Klagenfurth. I shall
write in greater detail from Udine."

On the morning of 16th March the divisions of Serurier,
Guieu, and Bernadotte were brought by short marches to
Passage   Valvasone, the point selected for the passage
of the   of the Tagliamento. The river was here no
Tagliamento more than two feet deep. At midday, covered
by the fire of their well-posted artillery, and protected by
islands and by the banks, the French troops entered the
stream, Serurier's division remaining in reserve. The
cavalry under Kellermann drove back the Austrian horse
and charged their guns. After some resistance, and having
The Arch-   lost 500 men and six guns, the Archduke
duke retreats Charles retired on Udine, and the French
occupied Gradisca. But before Napoleon could advance
on the road to Vienna it was necessary to drive the
Austrians from the right of his line of march. He accordingly sent Bernadotte in pursuit of the Archduke, who had
retired behind the Isonzo, and who had instructed General
Koblos to hold the pass of Tarvis. The remaining
French divisions under Guieu and Serurier occupied
Palmanuova.

Having established a strong post at this point, Napoleon
marched up the Isonzo, driving Bajalich and Ocskay before
him ; while the Archduke, followed by Bernadotte, retreated to Laybach and from thence up the valley of the
Save.

While these operations were in progress Joubert in the
Tyrol had acted on his instructions, had defeated and

destroyed the greater part of Davidovich's corps, and had driven it beyond the Brenner. He then stood at Lienz, **Joubert's** waiting to effect a junction with Napoleon **Movements** when his columns should have passed the Alps and entered the valley of the Drave.

Massena, in the meantime, pushed on up the Fella, a mountain torrent that poured from the heights of Tarvis **Massena** through a steep and rocky defile. On the 18th **reaches** March he was at Gemona ; on the 19th his **Tarvis** advanced guard cleared Ospedaletto of its defenders ; on the 20th they took the fort of Chiusa, climbing the heights above, and forcing the garrison to surrender by heaving rocks down on to the roof below. Next day the French soldiers, whose daring and enthusiasm no obstacles could deter, destroyed the *chevaux de frise* and other impediments erected by the defenders of the defile, and reached Pontafel. Still driving the defenders of the pass before him, Massena continued his advance. On the 23rd March he attacked the Austrians on the summit **Flight of the** of the pass at Tarvis, and after a stubborn **Austrians** fight, in which he lost some 900 men, drove them back, killing or wounding 600 and taking 1500 prisoners.

The Archduke Charles arrived late in the engagement, when the survivors were retreating, but could not stem the tide of demoralised men, who fled to Villach. Next day Bajalich made a counter-attack, but was defeated with a loss of 1600 men and six guns ; while later Koblos was forced to surrender with 500 men.

The Archduke now retired on Klagenfurth with the broken remains of his army. Napoleon with his other divisions joined Massena at Tarvis ; while Joubert, after some hard fighting, had advanced through Botzen and Brixen.

The Army of Italy had now reached the territory of their enemies after twelve months of desperate fighting, in Napoleon on which they had triumphed on every occasion. the Summit Not only the hostility of man but the forces of the Alps of nature had been encountered and overcome. The torrent-worn passes of the Apennines and the Alps, the rivers that poured from their recesses, sunless ravines, snow-capped and wind-swept heights had proved no obstacles to their enthusiasm, their valour, and their thirst for glory. And now the clangour of their trumpets resounded on the summit of the Alps, and proclaimed to an astonished world the advent of a genius that was in a few years to dominate the Continent of Europe. From those summits they looked down on the rich valley of Villach in the territory of their enemies, to which they descended on the 26th March 1797.

The Archduke was reorganising his shattered forces at Klagenfurth, between which place and Leudf he, on the 28th, took up a position to oppose the French advance. But his troops had neither the numbers nor the spirit to offer much resistance ; they retired before the French attack, and Napoleon and Massena entered Klagenfurth that evening. Napoleon now occupied the valley of the Drave ; the junction with Joubert was effected, and on the 30th March Massena pushed on to Saint Veit, driving the enemy before him.

On the 1st April the Austrians made a stand in the gorges in front of Neumarkt, but nothing could stop the Final stand *élan* of their enemies, who pierced their centre of the after a stubborn fight and drove them back Austrians to the Semmering Pass. Thus, driving the Austrians before him, Napoleon pressed on along the road to Vienna. But, although so far successful in the campaign that he had in his immediate front now no large organised force, he was not easy as to the general situation.

The Austrian Emperor had great resources; he still had a large army on the Rhine, and serious resistance would be opposed to Napoleon's march on the capital. The line of communication was ever lengthening, and using up more men as he advanced. The Tyrol was hostile; an Austrian force under Loudon had marched down the Adige; an insurrection had broken out in the Republic of Venice; the French communications were endangered.

On the 4th April the Austrians made a last stand at Judenberg, which was stormed and taken by the French **End of the** grenadiers. The Austrians had, however, had **War** enough of the war; on the 7th April, when the French advanced guard was already entering Leoben, the suspension of hostilities was signed at Judenberg by Napoleon and the plenipotentiaries of the Austrian Emperor.

On the 18th April the preliminaries of Leoben were signed by Napoleon on behalf of the French Republic. He had not awaited the arrival of General Clarke, the plenipotentiary of the Directory, who was hastening to the front from Turin. In view of the troubles in his rear, and the general situation detailed above, he was as anxious for the conclusion of peace as was the Austrian Emperor, and, self-reliant, and capable of taking a great responsibility, he agreed to terms which were not altogether pleasing to the Directory. These terms were subsequently ratified in the Treaty of Campo Formio.

Rapidly withdrawing his army, Napoleon posted it in the Venetian States; and within a month the oligarchy known as the Republic of Venice was a thing of the past

Napoleon has been criticised on the ground that he
adopted two distinct lines of operations in this
Comments   final phase of his campaign.   Let us see his
own reply to this criticism.

" Was not the march into Germany by two lines of
operations, those of the Tyrol and Pontebba, a violation
of the principle that an army should have but one line of
operations ?   Was not the junction of these two corps in
Carinthia, so far from the point of departure, contrary to
the principle of never uniting columns in the presence of
an enemy ?   Would it not have been better to have left
7000 or 8000 men on the defensive before Trent, and to
have collected 10,000 or 12,000 more upon the Piave ?
The necessity of operations in the Tyrol, a difficult theatre
of war, would thus have been avoided ; the plan would
not have been exposed to chances unfavourable for a
junction of the columns ; and at the opening of the campaign all forces would have been concentrated.

" Neither of these principles has been violated.   If only
8000 men had been left with Joubert on the Avicio, he
would have been attacked, and Davidovich would have
reached Verona before the French army arrived at Villach.
Joubert required at least 14,000 men in order to maintain
himself on the Avicio.   It seemed better to leave his forces
undiminished, thus giving him a superiority of force to
enable him to defeat Davidovich and drive him beyond
the Brenner.   The Tyrol is a difficult country, but fatal
to the vanquished.   The French had acquired a great
superiority over the German troops.

" Germany was not entered by two lines of operations,
since the Pusterthal is on the hither side of the summit of
the Alps, and so soon as Joubert had passed Lienz, the line
of operation was that of Villach and Pontebba. The junction

of the two corps was not effected in presence of the enemy, for when Joubert left Brixen to move to the right upon Spittal by the Pusterthal, or the valley of the Drave, the main army had reached Klagenfurth and had patrols as far as Lienz. The Archduke could not prevent this junction.

" Joubert remained on the defensive up to the time of the battle of the Tagliamento. After this battle he defeated and destroyed the greater part of Davidovich's corps, and drove it beyond the Brenner; and all this without risk, for if beaten, he would merely have fallen back from position to position in Italy. When he learnt that the army had passed the Julian Alps and the Drave, he made his movement to join by way of the Pusterthal, which was quite convenient. This operation, rapidly executed, was indeed in accordance with all rules; it should have had, and did have every advantage."

In this final phase of the campaign rapidity was essential to Napoleon, time was what his opponent required; the one to defeat the Austrian army before it could be largely reinforced, the other to gain time for reinforcements to arrive. From beginning to end the advance into Austria was masterly both in conception and execution; it showed Napoleon at his best, prepared to take the risks that were necessary to ensure decisive success, but in his dispositions eliminating the element of chance as far as possible.

His political acumen and his readiness to accept great responsibility were exhibited in the preliminaries of Leoben, as in the earlier phases of the campaign; for he was in a position to judge of the situation far better than the Directory. He possessed in the highest degree these qualities desirable but seldom found, of which one of our ablest military writers [1] has said :

Spencer Wilkinson.

" The best officers must be on the same intellectual level as the best men in the other professions and in public life. The men at the head of an army, the typical products of its corporate existence, ought to be intellectually and spiritually the peers of the leaders in other branches of life, on what Matthew Arnold called ' the first plane,' and in touch with the movement of national policy, and of literature, science and art.   Only on the first plane can any man be a statesman, and unless the chief men of an army are statesmen, a nation will fight its battles in vain The battles may be won, but the fruits of victory will be lost."

The ideal is a high one.   The general atmosphere of intellectual sterility, the dull routine of army life, the slow promotion by seniority under a system where mediocrity succeeds no less surely than brilliant attainments—these do not conduce to the production of men on the first plane as the typical products of the corporate existence of an army.   Only in great political cataclysms are men of character and talent likely to find a fair opportunity of rising professionally above the general dead-level.   As Napoleon said : " Revolutions are a favourable time for soldiers possessing courage and intellect."

It has been said that " only in despotisms are men in high offices chosen only for their fitness," a truism ex-emplified in the career of Napoleon Bonaparte, under whose ægis so brilliant a galaxy of military talent led the French conscripts to victory during twenty years of war.

Already, thus early in his career, the genius of the youthful general was fully recognised, and was feared by the Directory.   Well might they tremble to behold the influence of the man of whom General Clarke, their plenipotentiary in Italy, wrote from Milan in December 1796 :

" Here all regard him as a man of genius. He has great power over the soldiers of the Republican Army. His judgment is sure ; his resolutions are carried out with all his powers. His calmness amidst the most stirring scenes is as wonderful as his extraordinary rapidity in changing his plans if obliged to do so by unforeseen circumstances."

Added to all his other qualities he had, even thus early, a profound knowledge of human nature which assisted in his domination of those about him, and taught him that there are two levers for moving men, fear and self-interest, and led him to say later : " Men deserve the contempt with which they inspire me. I have only to put some gold lace on the coats of my virtuous republicans and they immediately become just what I wish them."

PART II

THE CAMPAIGN OF MARENGO, 1800

CHAPTER I

PREPARATIONS FOR THE CAMPAIGN

Napoleon and Oriental Conquest — The *Coup d'état* — General
Situation — Austrian Plans — French Plans — The Army of
Reserve — Massena at Genoa — The St Bernard Route—
Napoleon joins the Army — Composition of the Army of
Reserve—Situation in Italy—Comments

THE campaign in Italy had raised Napoleon to a pinnacle
of military glory such as no general since Frederick had
Napoleon   occupied in Europe.   More than this, the
and Oriental importance of his political position had been
Conquest   enhanced by the weakness of the Directory;
and his power and influence rested not only on his prestige
with the people, but on the devotion of that army which
in good time would be able to establish and support him
in the supreme authority of the State.   But the Directory
were not yet sufficiently discredited for a bold hand to
pluck at supreme power—the pear was not yet ripe.
With the conclusion of peace in Austria and the settlement of affairs in Italy, there was little left for Napoleon to
do in Europe ; for the maintenance of his position action,
war, was a necessity.

At this juncture his eyes turned towards the East, for,
as he said, " There is not enough of glory in this little

Europe; all great glory comes from there. . . . Only in the East have there ever been great empires and great cataclysms; in the East there are six hundred millions of human beings." He therefore undertook the expedition to Egypt in the spring of 1798, and, but for the failure before Acre, he might perhaps have accomplished his design of establishing an Oriental empire. But although marked by failure, the expedition to Egypt had great influence on the development of his character and therefore on his future career. His imagination was excited and inspired by the scenes around him, by the vastness of the East, by the Nile's enormous images; while his despotic nature was developed in a land where there was none to curb his ambitions. On the march to Cairo he said: " I saw myself freed from the fetters and constraints of civilisation; I dreamt all sorts of things, and saw the means of carrying out what I dreamt. I pictured myself on the road to Asia on an elephant, a turban on my head, and holding in my hand a new Koran, which I had written myself from my own inspiration. I would have combined in my enterprises the traditions of the two worlds, putting under contribution for my own advantage the whole domain of history; I would have attacked the British Empire in India, and restored my connection with old Europe by that conquest."

But the repulse before Acre dissipated these dreams, and he turned once more to Europe. At length he saw **The Coup** that the time had arrived for action in France, *d'état* where the incompetence of the Government had opened the way for the seizure of the helm of State by a strong and determined man, and had resulted in the loss of all that had been gained in the first campaign in Italy. Leaving behind him the futile visions of Oriental splendour that had for a brief space inspired his imagination, he returned to Paris, and on the 18th Brumaire (9th November 1799) established by a *coup d'état* the new form of Government, which gave him almost despotic power. As First Consul of the triumvirate he could direct policy, organise armies, and conduct campaigns.

During Napoleon's absence in Egypt war had again broken out between Austria, in alliance with Russia and General England, and France, but in Italy no success Situation had been met with by the French army, which had been driven back towards the sea in 1799. Moreau had held his own on the Rhine, and the veteran Russian general, Suvaroff, had been driven out of Switzerland, but in Italy the French held only Liguria. The opposing forces in Italy occupied, in the beginning of the year 1800, much the same general positions that they had held four years earlier, when Napoleon assumed command of the Army of Italy. Massena commanded 80,000 men on the line between Genoa and the Col di Tenda ; the passes of the Alps being held by another 10,000. The Austrian general Melas, a brave and able leader in spite of his seventy years, opposed him with 80,000 men in Piedmont, and 20,000 more in reserve in the garrisons of northern Italy. On the Rhine Moreau and the Austrian general Kray faced each other with equal armies of over 100,000 men.

The Austrian plan was for Kray to hold back Moreau on the Rhine, while Melas would destroy Massena or drive Austrian him out of Liguria, and invade Provence and Plans the Dauphiny, the English co-operating at a favourable moment by a descent on the French coast.

Napoleon for the first time found himself in a position French to direct the organisation of the military forces, Plans and the course of operations over the whole theatre of war, and in Berthier, now Minister, of War, he found a willing assistant. The First Consul, under the terms of the constitution, could not command an army in the field ; the command of the Army of Reserve that was to be formed at Dijon for the invasion of Italy was therefore given to Berthier, who was succeeded in the Ministry of War by Carnot.

A review of the situation pointed to the German theatre as the field for decisive operations ; the adoption of the offensive on the Rhine would, if resulting in success, open the road to Vienna, turn the Austrian position in Italy, and decide at once the fate of Austria. Broadly speaking, the first plan of campaign provided for the passage of the Rhine, and an advance on Stokach to drive the enemy beyond the Lech. As soon as the Army of the Rhine had pushed the Austrians back beyond Ulm, the reserve of that army was to cross the St Gothard and invade Italy, to be followed by the Army of Reserve which was to be assembled at Dijon. But this plan had no sooner been communicated to Moreau when information was received that Kray was manœuvring towards the Tyrol with a view to the eventual occupation of the Milanese, which Napoleon intended to take possession of. Moreover, Massena was being attacked in Genoa, where he could not long hold on to this last foothold of the French in Italy. To relieve him and to enable Suchet to assume the offensive from Nice, a diversion in the direction of Turin was necessary

A new plan was therefore formulated. Moreau, leaving a corps to guard Switzerland, was to operate on the right bank of the Rhine, and when he had obtained an advantage sufficient to establish a superiority over Kray, would detach a quarter of his army under Lecourbe,[1] who was to join the Army of Reserve under the orders of Berthier. The latter

[1] Afterwards replaced by Moncey.

would move to Geneva, posting a detachment under Moncey to guard Valais, while Moreau would hold the enemy's army in the Tyrol. Both armies would then undertake vigorous offensive operations, Berthier crossing the Alps, descending into Piedmont, and falling on the Austrian rear, while Moreau crossed the Rhine and invaded Austrian territory.

Early in March Napoleon instructed Massena to concentrate his forces at Genoa, and from that point to oppose the advance of the Austrians, telling him that " the enemy is sure to attack in three columns according to the Austrian mode ; you should avoid two of these columns and meet the third with all your strength."

Napoleon's principal difficulty lay at the outset in the formation of a fresh army for operations in Italy. For The Army of this purpose the Consuls ordered an extra-Reserve ordinary levy of 140,000 conscripts who were to form the Army of Reserve, of which Chabran's battalions at Chalons on the Saone would form a trained nucleus. Chabran's troops were in a state that recalls that of the Army of Italy when Napoleon assumed command of it in 1796 ; but ill-fed, ill-clothed, and lax in discipline though they were, they were ready to follow the First Consul to the ends of the earth. General Clarke, sent to inspect them, found only half effective, and all, including officers, in a state of penury.

From the time that a fresh campaign against the Austrians was decided upon, Napoleon worked unceasingly in preparing everything for the invasion of Piedmont. On the 1st March Berthier was directed to collect troops and provisions at Geneva, in a characteristic letter of instructions in which Napoleon entered into details with regard to the provision of ammunition, biscuits, brandy, cattle and mules. By March 30,000 men were assembled round Dijon; the artillery and train were organised at Auxonne. The difficulties to be overcome in the organisation of the army may be understood from the complaints of Chambarlhac, general of division at Dijon, and Chabran. The latter wrote to the First Consul on the 7th April :

" The troops are without pay. The officers are so much in arrears that they have no longer the means of subsistence. . . The results of this penury may be fatal. Insubordination would ensue if the officers, themselves subject to every kind of privation, did not display the most laudable zeal and firmness."

By the middle of April Massena, fighting with gallantry and skill, and thus gaining valuable time, had been driven
Massena at back by superior forces into Genoa, where he
Genoa was surrounded by 50,000 troops under Ott, and blockaded by the British fleet under Lord Keith ; while Suchet, with a portion of Massena's army, was driven back to Nice. The Austrians had advanced on three lines as Napoleon had predicted, and Massena had thus been able to make a more prolonged stand than he could have done had the enemy's masses been brought to bear against him simultaneously on the Napoleonic principle.

Napoleon had intended that the Army of Reserve should cross into Italy by the Simplon or the St Gothard, but this
The news from Genoa and Moreau's inaction decided
St Bernard him to take the route of the St Bernard. He
Route had been told that this route was impracticable ; but the man who had dreamt of following in the footsteps of Alexander of Macedon to " plant the new

pillars of Hercules on the bank of the Hydaspes," was not likely to falter in an undertaking that, twenty centuries before, had been accomplished by Hannibal. On the 27th April he wrote to Berthier :

" We may possibly be unable to go to Milan, but shall have to march to Tortona for the relief of Massena, who, if defeated, will shut himself up in Genoa, where he has thirty days' supplies. I wish, therefore, to cross by the St Bernard."

General Marescot, who had surveyed the pass, reported that the passage, though difficult and dangerous, was practicable. The men who could accomplish it would merit the title of the first soldiers in the world. Descending the valley of the Aosta, they would drive out the few Austrian troops posted there, and fall on the rear of Melas' army in Italy. Suchet was in the meantime directed to hold the line of the Var, and to offer a stubborn resistance to the Austrian advance.

At daybreak on the 6th May 1800 Napoleon, enveloped in a long grey coat, and accompanied by his secretary, **Napoleon** Bourrienne, descended the staircase of the **joins the** Tuileries, entered his carriage and was driven **Army** rapidly through Paris. That day he drove fifteen hours to Auxonne, occupying himself *en route* with plans and papers. Next day he reached Dijon, where he inspected Chambarlhac's and Boudet's divisions, the condition of which had not greatly improved. The soldiers were not yet fully armed, clothed and equipped. He stirred up the commissary, who had neglected his duties, harangued the soldiers, who were inspired by his presence, and, inspecting workshops and gun-foundries *en route*, arrived at Geneva on the 8th May to direct the advance of the army across the Alps.

H

Composition of the Army of Reserve   The Army of Reserve, now ⁓in Switzerland or on the road thither, was constituted as follows :—

	Men
I. Corps (Advanced Guard), Lannes . .	9500
(Including Watrin's Division of 5800 and Rivaud's Cavalry, 1100)	
II. Corps, Duhesme	14,500
Boudet's Division, 7300	
Loison's Division, 7200	
III. Corps, Victor	18,700
Monnier's Division, 5800	
Chambarlhac's Division, 7900	
Chabran's Division, 5000	
IV. Corps (Cavalry), Murat . .	7000
Artillery, Marmont, 76 guns and . .	1100
Consular Guard	400
Auxiliary service, train, muleteers, artificers, hospital, etc.	2500

In addition, Moncey's division of 15,000, which Moreau had been ordered to detach from the Army of the Rhine, was moving towards the St Gothard with a view to occupying the left bank of the Ticino as far as Lugano, and the Mont Cenis was held by a force of 3000 men under Turreau, who was later to advance on Susa. Chabran's division was in Savoy, ready to cross by the Little St Bernard and join Lannes at Aosta. Dupont was Chief of the Staff.

Napoleon did not forget to provide for all possible eventualities. A second army of reserve was formed at Dijon, and militia were employed in guarding the line of communication through Switzerland as the army advanced

On the 12th May Napoleon proceeded to Lausanne, between which place and Villeneuve four divisions were Situation in posted along the Lake of Geneva, with the Italy in May advanced guard at Martigny in the Rhone valley. He had already, when at Dijon, received from Massena's envoy, Franceschi, who had only escaped the English ships by swimming ashore with his sabre in his mouth, a terrible account of the straits to which the French in Genoa were reduced. Now he had later news by a messenger who had left Genoa on the last day in April, and heard that the town, while subjected to a terrible bombardment, was almost reduced to starvation. Massena with 28,000 men, including 16,000 sick and wounded, was now shut up in the fortress of Genoa, besieged by General Ott with 24,000 men. Melas with 28,000 had driven Suchet, who commanded Massena's left wing of 10,000 men, along the Riviera coast across the French frontier. At Lausanne also he had news that Moreau had beaten Kray at Stokach and Mæskirch. The time had arrived to advance.

On the 16th May Napoleon left Lausanne; on the 17th he reached Martigny. Lannes' advanced guard had already started in favourable weather; the violent storms of the few previous days had ceased, and the sun shone. It was warm at the foot of the mountains which raised their snow-capped summits and rugged peaks far above the advancing army.

The first conception of a campaign in Germany, had it proved feasible, was undoubtedly the one that offered most chances of decisive success. Had the Comments French army in overwhelming strength—that is, Moreau's army reinforced by the Army of Reserve—marched on Vienna, there need have been no campaign in Italy, and Napoleon could have dictated the terms of peace at Vienna.

But Moreau was obstructive, and none but Napoleon was capable of carrying this plan to a successful issue. Moreau would not serve under Napoleon, and the latter did not as yet occupy a sufficiently secure position to enable him to coerce his lieutenant.

When that plan proved impossible, we find Napoleon at once conceiving the daring project of crossing the Alps, which, in assuring the surprise of the enemy, fulfilled one of the first principles of war. Having decided on a campaign in Italy, he chose the route which, while nearest to his own base of operations, would enable him to debouch into that country at the most favourable point for the attainment of his first object—the relief of Genoa.

CHAPTER II

The Great St Bernard—March of the Advanced Guard—The Fort of Bard—Napoleon crosses the Alps—Comments

RISING to a height of 8111 feet, the Great St Bernard Pass offers the most direct route from Geneva to Milan. The **The Great** road leaves the valley of the Rhine at Martigny, **St Bernard** and, after traversing the Alps, enters that of the Dora Baltea at Aosta, a distance of fifty-three miles. On the summit of the pass, thirty-two miles from Martigny, stands, and has stood for nearly a thousand years, the hospice of St Bernard, established for the assistance of travellers in those wild and inhospitable regions.

Even in summer the cold on the Alps is excessive. The country is mainly characterised by barren rocks and masses of snow and ice, and is destitute of trees. It was over this rugged way that Napoleon determined to carry his army for the reconquest of Italy.

The advanced guard under Lannes left San Moritz on the 13th May, and rapidly mounted the ever-ascending **March of the** road, on either side of which the snow-clad **Advanced** Alps rose higher as they advanced. There **Guard** were great columns and precipices of granite, masses of snow ready to fall in avalanches down the mountain-side, glaciers which poured forth icy torrents, and dark and threatening clouds that presaged storm upon their summits. Soon the road wound along the bed of the

Dranse torrent, which flows from the St Bernard, and the advanced guard entered the town of Martigny. At midday a storm came on, and drenched the toiling troops, who were half frozen by the icy wind. The inhabitants of the villages through which they passed deserted their dwellings and fled on the approach of the French column, and the Valaisans were generally unfriendly and unwilling to furnish supplies. Some had been employed under Marescot in improving the road, but were with difficulty restrained from deserting. That night the advanced guard halted at St Pierre, on the right bank of the Dranse. Provisions had been collected at various points *en route*, a hospital had been established here, and Marmont had already proceeded with the guns in the direction of St Bernard ; supplies for the troops were conveyed on mules. But by the time the cavalry, which brought up the rear, arrived at St Pierre, there were no supplies left, and the famished men broke into the deserted houses and helped themselves.

The advanced guard continued up the course of the Dranse on the 14th ; at midday Lannes issued the following instructions :—

" The advanced guard will pass the Great St Bernard on the night of the 25th-26th floréal (15th-16th May), whatever difficulties they may meet with. The head of the column will leave the Proz valley at midnight. The men will be in two ranks ; the mounted officers will be on foot, leading their horses. No one is to cry or call out for fear of causing the fall of avalanches. Where the way is difficult the soldiers are authorised to support themselves with their muskets. No one will be allowed to quit the road that has been marked out. Fifty lanterns will be distributed among the demi-brigades to light the march of the troops as far as the hospice. General Marescot will place between battalions pontoon corps men who can construct bridges over the Dranse in case of necessity.

" Every man will carry a ration of biscuit. Peasants of St Pierre and mules will be laden with supplies.

" On arriving at the hospice, the 6th Light Demi-brigade will receive some provisions from the monks, will pass the artillery and rapidly advance on the Austrian posts. When the enemy has been driven from his positions, the demi-brigade will march as quickly as possible on Aosta, which must be taken at all costs.

" The Commander-in-chief of the advanced guard appeals to the devotion of the soldiers of the Republic to force a passage regarded by the enemy as inaccessible. Twenty centuries have passed since the Carthaginian soldiers forced it to go and fight the Roman legions. Europe will be stupefied on hearing that we have marched with guns and baggage on the tracks of those heroes.

" Officers and soldiers, Frenchmen whom no dangers can appal, the First Consul places his confidence in your courage. Do not forget, at the moment when you march against the enemy, that your brothers-in-arms await in Genoa, in the midst of the most terrible sufferings from famine, the deliverance which you will bring them after traversing Piedmont and Lombardy."

As indicated in these instructions, Marmont's artillery had preceded the advanced guard and, dragged up by the unwilling peasants of Valais, reached the St Bernard on the 18th. Dismounted from their carriages and placed in the hollowed trunks of pine-trees, the guns were hauled up, the wheels and other component parts being carried by the men.

With difficulty and some loss the men toiled on up the

rugged way; at one point an avalanche broke from the heights above, and overwhelmed some hapless soldiers in fifty feet of snow.   At length, having overcome all the perils and difficulties of the ascent, the advanced guard stood triumphant on the summit of the St Bernard on the morning of the 16th May.   Lannes had carried out the orders given him on the 10th May, to pass the St Bernard an hour before dawn on the 16th.   Here provisions were furnished by the monks of the hospice, with whom arrangements had already been made by Napoleon.

There had been since 1798 a small French garrison at the hospice.   In April they were attacked by an Austrian column from Saint Remy, but with musketry and the fire of two small guns the French easily held their own, and repulsed the assailants with loss.   After this the Austrians remained in observation, having a battalion at Etroubles with a detachment at Saint Remy, and a considerable force at Aosta, farther down the valley.

Arrived at the hospice of St Bernard, no time was lost in continuing the advance according to the instructions that had been issued.   The 6th Light Demi-brigade, having been served with bread, cheese, and wine, passed to the front and, supported by four guns, took the Austrians at Saint Remy by surprise and drove them down the steep declivity of the valley below.   Lannes with his Staff followed, and by the time he arrived at the foot of the mountain the 6th were already on the road to Aosta. The remainder of Watrin's division and the guns followed. The French pressed on ; the Austrians were driven from Etroubles, and across the bridge over the Buttier, which they had not time to destroy.   Leaving that place, the 6th marched down the right bank of the Buttier, and arrived before Aosta, which was entered after a short resistance by the enemy, who occupied the walls.

The remainder of the division now came on, and encamped on either side of the road to Turin beyond the town. Here Lannes halted to await the arrival of Chabran, who descended from the Little St Bernard on the afternoon of the 17th May. The cavalry of Rivaud's brigade, which had followed the infantry of the advanced guard at a day's interval, had made a double march, and also came up at this point. A post was established at Saint Remy.

Lannes wasted no time. Napoleon had given the 10th June as the date by which the army should arrive before Genoa for the relief of Massena. The advanced guard moved on down the valley ; on the 18th May Chatillon was taken, after a stout resistance by 1200 Austrians who, with thirteen guns, occupied an intrenched position. But Watrin sent some infantry to storm the town, turning the position on both flanks at the same time ; and the Austrians retreated in the direction of Ussel with the loss of 500 men and two guns, the French losing only about a hundred men. In this action the cavalry of the advanced guard bore a distinguished part.

The advanced guard was now brought to a standstill before the fort of Bard, which blocked the outlet of the The Fort valley of Aosta, a narrow defile between the of Bard Monte Iseran and the Monte Rosa. On the 20th May Berthier wrote to the First Consul :

" The castle of Bard is a greater obstacle than we thought, for it is impossible to get the artillery past it until we have taken it. The infantry and cavalry can turn it by taking a mule-track from Armaz to Perlo."

Lannes occupied the heights above this formidable obstacle, and set to work to improve the track over the Albaredo mountain on the left of Bard, for the passage of

the infantry and cavalry.   But he could not push on down
the Dora Baltea into Piedmont without artillery, in the
face of a large hostile force with guns; and his supplies
would not last more than a few days.   No supplies were
obtainable in the valley, and there were no means at hand
for the construction of batteries.

In the meantime the remaining divisions were pressing
on in rear; by the 22nd the whole army would be across
the Alps, and here was all progress stopped by this little
fort, with its 400 defenders and their forty-five guns.
Jomini gives the following description of it :—

" The rock of Bard is a fragment of Mount Albaredo
which closes the valley.   The fort, constructed in an
ellipse, conforms to the shape of the rock, with several
towers and batteries protected from superior fire from the
rocks of Albaredo.   Galleries communicate between the
advanced batteries and the upper fort. . . . Its works
enfilade from a distance the street of the town of Bard."

It was time for Napoleon to push on to the front, in
order to overcome this obstruction to the forward march of
his army.

We left the First Consul at Martigny, where he had
arrived on the 17th May.   On the 20th he left that place,
Napoleon   and at St Pierre exchanged his horse for a mule,
crosses the   on which he rode up the St Bernard.   On the
Alps   way his mule stumbled and threw him, but the
muleteer saved him from falling down the precipice below
the road.   His impatience at the delay at Bard was evident.
At each halt he inquired eagerly if there were despatches
from Berthier.   Bourrienne[1] says: "He wore his grey coat,
and walked with his whip in his hand, in a somewhat

[1] His private secretary.

melancholy mood, because none brought him news of the surrender of the fort of Bard." He dined at the hospice, stayed there for a time, inspected the place and its surroundings, turning over in the library the leaves of a book containing an account of Hannibal's passage of the Alps. At half-past six in the evening, after thanking the monks for their hospitality, he left the hospice, sent his horse on to Saint Remy, and at one point, to avoid a detour of the road, sat down and slid a distance of a hundred metres down the snow-covered declivity. At nine o'clock he reached Etroubles, where he stayed the night, before continuing the journey to Aosta. There he halted several days. On the 24th he rode over to Bard, narrowly escaping an Austrian cavalry patrol, by whom he was held up ; but with great presence of mind he kept the officer in conversation until his own escort came up, and made prisoners of the patrol.

At Bard Napoleon surveyed the fort from the summit of Albaredo. It was attacked next morning, but the assailants were repulsed with the loss of 200 men. It was necessary to get the guns through. Lannes had gone on with his infantry and cavalry, who had crossed the Albaredo mountain. That night a heavy storm came on. The wheels of the guns and their carriages were wrapped round with hay and straw, the road was strewn with the same material ; at midnight, in the midst of torrential rain, the guns were thus dragged along the road below the fort of Bard, sixty men to each. Not until the last carriage was passing did the garrison become aware of what was happening ; too late they threw down burning fire-balls, and directed a heavy fire of shot and shell on the way below. But the guns had passed, and were already on the way to join Lannes, who captured Ivrea before they reached him

The main army had already begun to pass across the mountain. By the 26th they had all passed, leaving a force under Andreossy to carry on the siege of Bard. The passage of the Alps was accomplished, and Napoleon with 50,000 men descended into the plains of Piedmont. The gallant defenders of Bard, under Captain Bernkopf, held out until the 2nd June, when, a breach having been made in the walls and an assault being imminent, they surrendered as prisoners of war.

In the execution of the plan of crossing the St Bernard, the driving force which carried the army over the Alps is

Comments visible at every point, overcoming all difficulties, telling Berthier that "with time and trouble no obstacles are insurmountable." To Napoleon there was no such word as impossible.

Some critics have contended that Napoleon undertook great risks in his passage of the Alps; that while in its broad conception his plan was masterly, his neglect to consider details endangered its success. But it is the mark of a great commander to know just what risks can be taken to secure a great success. "The mind that is constantly occupied with small things commonly becomes incapable of great ones." Napoleon conceived his plans always in their broadest aspect, knowing well that he would be able to settle details during the course of execution of his plans. He had sufficient confidence in himself to be sure of his ability to cope with and overcome obstacles whenever they might arise. So long as the plan was correctly outlined in its broad strategical features, the details might be left to be filled in as circumstances developed. These are the surest signs of a great general who is able to concentrate thought and effort to the attainment of the main object.

It was the inspiration, the force of character, and the prestige of the great commander under whom they served that enabled those under him to accomplish so much. When his troops turned the fort of Bard by crossing the Albaredo mountain, he wrote :

" Fifteen hundred men worked with activity to render practicable a road over the Albaredo. Where the fall was too steep, ladders were constructed ; where the path was too narrow, where it was bounded on the right or left by a precipice, walls were raised to prevent men from falling ; where the rocks were separated by deep gulfs, bridges were thrown across to reunite them ; and, across a mountain regarded for centuries as inaccessible for infantry, the French cavalry has effected a passage."

It was the concentrated energy of the great commander that pushed the army, with the loss of three men, over the pass which Hannibal had crossed with difficulty and with the loss of thousands.

CHAPTER III

Napoleon reviews the Situation—The French Advance—Movements of Melas—The Advance to Milan—Fall of Genoa—The Conquest of Lombardy—The Battle of Montebello—Dispositions of the French—Comments

On the 24th May, Napoleon, reviewing the situation, wrote :

" The enemy appears to be surprised by our movement. He is at a loss what to do, and as yet scarcely credits it. **Napoleon** On the 18th May, the Austrians were posted **reviews the** as follows :—12,000 at Nice, 6000 at Savona **Situation** and on the Genoese Riviera, 25,000 before Genoa, 8000 at Susa and Pignerol, 3000 at Romano, Ivrea and Bard, 8000 facing the Simplon and the St Gothard, 5000 on the side of Acqui and in Lombardy. The enemy remained in these positions until our arrival at Ivrea. 3000 men who were in this valley have been beaten and dispersed. The corps which was about Susa has taken up a position between Turin and Ivrea. Nice is probably evacuated by now."

Lannes remained at Ivrea on the 25th, reconnoitring in the direction of Turin ; the Austrians under Haddick were **The French** holding the bridge over the Chiusella with 5000 **Advance** men and fifty guns, and had 4000 cavalry in rear towards Chivasso. The Austrian commander thought he had only a French division to deal with, not dreaming that a great army had crossed the Alps.

On the 26th Napoleon joined Lannes at Ivrea, and the advance was continued down the Dora Baltea towards Turin. In the face of a heavy artillery fire Watrin's division drove the Austrians back, and seized the Chiusella bridge near Romano. Napoleon was present during this action, and at one time in such close contact with the enemy that he and his staff drew their swords to defend themselves. The French cavalry pursued as far as Chivasso, where Lannes remained in observation while the army was assembled about Ivrea

Melas had for some time refused to believe that a French army had crossed the Alps. He had been led to expect **Movements** that some troops were advancing from the **of Melas** Simplon and Mont Cenis, where demonstrations had been made by Turreau, but he had declared the Army of Reserve to be a phantom. When he had news of General Haddick's defeat, while a cavalry officer told him that he had recognised Napoleon himself in the action at Romano, he was obliged to accept the fact that the First Consul had entered Piedmont at the head of a large army. Leaving Nice and arresting the advance of his troops into Provence, he repassed the Col di Tenda and hurried to Turin, where he arrived on the 29th May. There he collected some eight thousand men, while he sent directions to Ott to raise the siege of Genoa and march on Alessandria.

Hitherto Napoleon had been marching on Turin. He now conceived the plan of changing the direction of his **The Advance** march to Milan, where he would be in a **to Milan** position to dominate the whole of Lombardy and to place himself across the Austrian lines of communication south of the Po. But before concentrating to the south of the Po it was necessary to clear Lombardy of the Austrians, who might otherwise concentrate on his flanks and rear. He must clear the left bank of the Po and the country between Brescia and Cremona, when, crossing the Po, he could advance through Piacenza to the relief of Genoa. The Austrian generals, Loudon and Wukassovich, were gathering troops on the Ticino.

The French order of march was now changed. Lannes' advanced guard together with Chambarlhac's division became a right flank guard, standing for the present at Chivasso, where it covered the army from the direction of Turin. Turreau operated in the valley of the Susa; Murat, forming the new advanced guard, drove the Austrians out of Vercelli, and occupied that place; followed by Duhesme with the divisions of Loison and Boudet. From Vercelli Murat turned towards Milan, the road south towards Casale having been cleared by Duhesme, who then returned to Vercelli. Chabran was still in the valley of Aosta, Monnier guarded Ivrea, and Moncey reached Bellinzona on the 29th May. On the 30th Murat was at Novara, the Austrians under Wukassovich retreating in front of him and taking up a position at Turbigo on the Ticino, while Loudon was at Pavia.

Lannes was now directed to march on Pavia. Murat and Duhesme forced the passage of the Ticino, and drove the Austrians back on Milan, whence they retreated eastwards before the French advance. On the 2nd June Murat entered Milan, and was followed two hours later by the First Consul himself.

Melas now at length became aware of his danger, and directed the march of all his available troops on Alessandria.

In the meantime Massena was reduced to the last extremity at Genoa. But Ott had received orders to raise the siege, and join the general concentration at Alessandria, where the Austrians would have to fight for existence. He could only delay long enough to come to terms with Fall of Genoa Massena, who was allowed to march out with all the honours of war, a portion of his force to join Suchet and the rest to be conveyed in British ships to Antibes. This was on the 4th June. Next day Ott set out for Alessandria at the head of 15,000 men.

On arrival at Milan, into which he made a triumphant entry in a carriage drawn by six white horses on 2nd June, The Conquest of Lombardy Napoleon despatched Duhesme and Murat against the Austrians, under Wukassovich, who were gathering strength on the Lambro. From there the Austrians were driven back on the 8rd June, when the French occupied Melegnano, after some severe fighting. The French followed them next day to Lodi, where the retreating enemy offered little resistance, blew up the bridge after crossing the Adda, and retired on Crema.

Loison, with his division of 7000 men, some cavalry and guns, was now sent to Brescia to clear Eastern Lombardy and protect the French rear when the army should wheel to the west. Duhesme marched down the Adda to Crema, which he took after some hard fighting, and there Loison rejoined him after having accomplished his task. Murat at the same time accupied Piacenza, on the 6th June.

Napoleon had meanwhile remained at Milan, occupied with political matters, and awaiting the arrival of Moncey, who reached that place on the 7th June, when the army was concentrating on Piacenza and Stradella. Moncey was directed to hold Milan and to operate in Eastern Lombardy with a portion of his force. Part of his corps was, however, formed into a division under

I

Gardanne, and joined Lannes during the advance on Marengo.

It was not until the 8th June that Napoleon learnt of the fall of Genoa from an intercepted despatch written by Melas at Turin on the 5th.   This despatch also detailed the movements of the various Austrian Corps, and stated that Ott was leaving Genoa for Voghera on the morning of the 6th.   From this information the First Consul judged that the Austrians could not concentrate their forces at Alessandria before the 12th or 13th.   He accordingly wrote to Berthier :

" Let the divisions advance boldly and destroy all the troops they encounter.   The vanguard may advance as far as Voghera."

Lannes marched from Pavia on the morning of the 9th, followed by Victor's corps and Chambarlhac's division. **The Battle of** The Austrian general, Ott, was making for **Montebello** Stradella in hopes of opposing the French passage of the Po at that point.   Lannes heard of Ott's arrival at Casteggio, where the Austrians occupied the heights in front of the town.   The French general was fearless and enterprising, and had that confidence in himself which is one of the surest factors in victory.   His men were impatient to engage the enemy.   Crossing the Po, he attacked the enemy without awaiting the arrival of Victor's divisions.   A fierce fight ensued.   Watrin's division was at first forced back by superior numbers, and was only saved from defeat by the arrival of Chambarlhac, who attacked the enemy's right flank, while Lannes assailed their centre, and the Austrians were driven back to Castelnuovo with a loss of 5000 men and five guns.   The French lost heavily.   It was in this action that the grenadier

Coignet saved his captain and killed eight Austrians with his own hand. The cavalry under Rivaud, a young brigadier, twenty-four years of age, bore a distinguished part in the battle, and killed or wounded 1500 of the enemy; had a large force of cavalry been available it is probable that Ott's entire army would have been destroyed. Napoleon had left Milan that morning, and, riding through Pavia and Stradella, arrived when the battle was over, and established his headquarters at the latter place. The road to Alessandria was now open.

On the 10th June, then, while the Austrians were concentrating at Alessandria, Napoleon had at his disposal **Dispositions** for battle only some 30,000 men out of the **of the** 65,000 who had crossed the Alps. Moncey was **French** at a distance, holding Milan and clearing the country between the Oglio and the Chiesa. Duhesme and Loison with 6000 men were at Cremona, and Chabran at Vercelli. On the 11th the remainder of the army was gathered between Casteggio and Voghera. Murat and Boudet came in from Piacenza; Monnier reached Stradella; Desaix, who had arrived from Egypt, was given command of Monnier's and Boudet's divisions.

It will be observed that the boldness of Napoleon's plan developed as he advanced. At first a movement on Turin, **Comments** and then direct to Genoa for the relief of **Comments** Massena sufficed to satisfy his ambition. Piedmont and Lombardy could be conquered when Genoa had been relieved The project of placing his army astride of the Austrian lines of communication, there to give battle and end the campaign at one blow, was simple indeed in conception, but required the courage and resolution of genius to carry it to a successful issue But it was ever the habit of Napoleon to plan campaigns with a view to decisive victory, and in Marengo we see a presage of those great campaigns of Austerlitz and Jena, where the fate of empires was decided by a single blow.

The manner in which Lombardy was swept from end to end by the ordered movement of the different forces which then wheeled round to the west and faced the Austrians at Marengo is worthy of notice.

CHAPTER IV

THE BATTLE OF MARENGO

Preliminary Movements—Battle of Marengo—Results of
the Campaign—Comments

In the concentration Melas had been no more successful
than his adversary. His troops were scattered ; Loudon
Preliminary and Wukassovich had been driven to the
Movements Mincio. A large force was engaged in opposing
Suchet, and a garrison had to be left in Genoa. Of the
100,000 men under his command in Northern Italy, the
Austrian Commander-in-Chief had collected only some
29,000 infantry and 9000 cavalry at Alessandria. He had
115 guns to the French 38.

The forward movement of the French army continued
on the 12th, Gardanne's division forming the advanced
guard. Napoleon went to Voghera, and ordered a bridge
to be constructed across the Po near its junction with the
Scrivia, to establish communication with the left bank,
where Chabran was moving between Vercelli and Pavia.
The remainder of the army was echeloned between
Voghera and the Scrivia. A detachment watched Tortona,
held by an Austrian garrison.

Next day Napoleon crossed the Scrivia, and entered the
plain of Marengo, where he had expected to encounter his
adversary, for whose superior cavalry the country afforded
a favourable field of action. The garrison of Castelnuovo
was driven out and retired on Alessandria, leaving 2000

133

sick and wounded.   A force, with guns, was åt S. Giuliano-vecchio, but these also retired when a French battery was established to oppose them.   Ott deployed his forces about Marengo, and a sharp engagement ensued, which ended in the Austrians retiring across the Bormida.

That night the French forces were disposed as follows :— Gardanne and Victor's corps in and between Marengo and the Fontanone ; Lannes and Murat at San Giulianovecchio and round Castel Ceriolo ; Monnier in rear at Torre di Garofolo, where the First Consul had his headquarters.

The movements of the Austrians in retirement had led Napoleon to believe that they had abandoned the intention of advancing from Alessandria through Marengo.   He was at a loss to know what were Melas' plans, but thinking that a battle was no longer imminent, he detached Desaix with Boudet's division towards Novi to see if the Austrians were advancing in that direction, while Rivaud's cavalry were sent towards Salé to watch the lower Tanaro.

The Austrians had, however, remained in Alessandria, and had thrown three bridges across the Bormida opposite Pietrabona, which were not discovered by their opponents, owing to bad reconnoitring work.   Napoleon was therefore led to expect that if Melas was advancing, his movement must be towards one flank or other.   That night, the 13th June, Melas held a council of war, and decided to attack the French next day.   His troops were echeloned in lines behind the Bormida, no fires being allowed for fear of betraying their position to the enemy.

The plain of Marengo was covered with vineyards, corn-fields, and pasture land, intersected by lanes and hedges, **The** and dotted with farms and hamlets   After **Battlefield** passing the defile of San Giuliano the road to Tortona bifurcated, one branch crossing the Bormida above Marengo, the other leading north-west to Alessandria.

From this point a road ran through Castel Ceriolo to Salé. The tract of country between Marengo and the Bormida was generally marshy. Midway between the Bormida and the defile of San Giuliano the plain rose with a gentle slope, and formed a plateau overlooked by a round hill near San Giuliano.

" The framework of the battlefield was the most southerly road from Tortona to Alessandria, and the road from Alessandria to Salé. It formed a quadrilateral figure of unequal sides, the western angles being Marengo and Castel Ceriolo, and the eastern angles San Giuliano and La Ghilina. The main conflict took place between the old road to Tortona, and the cross-road from Castel Ceriolo to La Ghilina." [1]

The Austrian plan of attack provided for the establishment, under cover of an advanced guard, of two batteries **Austrian** in front of Marengo, under protection of which **Plan of** O'Reilly would advance with 3000 infantry and **Attack** some cavalry against La Spinetta. Ott with 8000 infantry and d'Elnitz' cavalry was to turn the French right by way of Castel Ceriolo. The Austrian main body would in the meantime deploy on the Marengo plain. When these operations had developed, Melas would attack the French centre with 20,000 men and 100 guns.

The Austrian advanced guard passed the Bormida at daybreak on the 14th June, and at 7 o'clock O'Reilly's **Battle of** brigade drove the French outposts from the **Marengo** farm of Pietrabona, and, together with the guns, engaged Gardanne's division. But the latter, although surprised, checked O'Reilly, and took up a strong position behind the Marengo stream, while Chambarlhac's division reinforced their right.

[1] Hooper.

By half-past eight the greater part of the Austrian army had passed the Bormida, and the attack was concentrated against Marengo, the key of the position.   But Lannes had also arrived at Marengo, and, after fierce fighting in front of that place, the Austrian attack was checked.   The arrival of Watrin's division, which took post on the right of the village, obliged the Austrians to retreat.   They had been driven back in three desperate attacks.

But now the overwhelming fire of the Austrian artillery was more than the French could stand against, and at one o'clock their line in front of Marengo was broken; they had run short of ammunition and they were obliged to fall back.   At the same time Ott had entered Castel Ceriolo, and attacked Lannes' right flank.   O'Reilly assailed the left of their line, and the fire of eighty and afterwards of a hundred guns was brought to bear upon the centre, which was driven far back beyond Marengo, Lannes being obliged to conform to this movement.

Napoleon, who had ridden to the field of action, saw the precarious situation of his army.   He sent Monnier's division to reinforce his right, and threw his bodyguard into the battle; but, although these troops delayed the Austrians for a time, they could make no headway against the superior numbers of the enemy, supported as they were by the fire of a hundred guns.   A retreat was ordered, and the Austrian Commander-in-Chief, thinking that the victory was secure, rode back to Alessandria, leaving the conduct of the pursuit to General Zach, his Chief of the Staff.   But Zach was slow.   Instead of continuing the pursuit at once, he delayed to make fresh dispositions, and to reform his army.   In the meantime Napoleon had ascended the clock tower of San Giulianonuovo, and from there he saw Desaix's troops rapidly approaching between San Giulianovecchio and Rivalta.   As already

related, Desaix had been despatched in the direction
of Novi with Boudet's division ; but immediately he
heard of the Austrian advance, Napoleon sent to recall
him.

It was four o'clock.   The battle appeared to be lost, but
the French were retiring steadily, Kellermann covering
the right with his cavalry, and arrangements had been
made to replenish their ammunition.   The slowness of the
Austrian pursuit enabled Berthier to halt at 4.30. Napoleon
ordered the formation of a fresh line of battle in rear of the
Buschetta.   The troops were turned about.   Desaix took
up a position in front of San Giulianovecchio ; the remainder of the army formed up on either flank, and 11,000
French infantry were again in line.   Fire had ceased ; the
First Consul rode along the lines of divisions crying :
" Soldiers ! recollect that I am accustomed to sleep on the
field of battle."

Marmont formed a battery of eighteen guns, which he
charged with grape and established on a mound on Desaix's
right ; Kellermann gathered together 1200 cavalry, and
took post in rear of the battery.

Meanwhile Zach, having formed his troops into two great
columns at an interval of two miles, with his cavalry in the
plain on the left, advanced up the Piacenza road with
drums beating and colours flying.   He saw the French
line halted, but marched on with confidence, and neglected
to establish his batteries, which were so vastly superior
to the French artillery.   Suddenly the French infantry
opened a devastating fire on the head of the column,
charged with the bayonet and drove the leading battalion
back upon the remainder, and at the same moment the
thunder of Marmont's guns burst upon the right, the grape
opening a great gap in the left of the Austrian column.
Napoleon sent an aide-de-camp to order a cavalry charge,

and Kellermann, having advanced to the right of the guns, struck the Austrians in flank, where the batteries had broken them, cut right through them, capturing Zach and 4000 prisoners. He then took to the right, after re-assembling his squadrons, and drove the Austrian cavalry from the field.

A general advance took place; the remaining Austrians were driven headlong back; Marengo and Castel Ceriolo were retaken. Ott attempted to penetrate the French left, but had to retreat for fear of being surrounded. Some battalions made a short stand at La Spinetta, but were attacked by infantry, charged by Kellermann's cavalry, and driven across the Bormida. Melas, who had returned to the field of battle, was one of the last to recross the river, and by eight o'clock not a living Austrian, except prisoners and wounded, remained on the field of Marengo, now re-occupied by the French. The French loss was heavy, amounting to over five thousand men, and Desaix was killed, but never was victory more complete. Of the fine Austrian army that crossed the Bormida in the morning, not more than 10,000 remained to take their places in the ranks.

The campaign which terminated in the battle of Marengo was decisive in its effects. Next morning **Results** Melas sent a flag of truce to ask for an **of the** armistice. Under the terms agreed upon **Campaign** the French recovered Lombardy and Pied-mont; the Austrians retired behind the Mincio, retaining some places to the south of the Po. The French army occupied the country between the Chiesa, the Oglio, and the Po. The tract between the Chiesa and the Mincio was to be neutral territory. The suspension of hostilities was to continue, pending the receipt of a reply from Vienna, but in case of a resumption of the war, ten days' notice was to be given before either army attacked the other.

This campaign broke the power of Austria in Italy, although peace was not concluded until the treaty of Lunéville, eight months later, when Moreau had gained the battle of Hohenlinden.

Napoleon returned to Milan, making a triumphal entry amid the acclamations of the inhabitants, directed the reorganisation of the army, the command of which was given to Massena, and on the 26th June set out for Paris, the Austrian Emperor having ratified the convention concluded after the battle of Marengo. The First Consul passed through Turin, over the Mont Cenis to Lyons, where he received an ovation from the populace. On the 2nd July the conqueror re-entered Paris, which he had quitted less than two months before.

It is difficult to understand why Napoleon did not assemble all his available forces to oppose the Austrian advance from Alessandria, in accordance with his own principle that every available man should be assembled on the day of battle. It seems probable that this neglect to concentrate was largely due to overweening confidence ; numerical superiority was all the more necessary in view of his inferiority in artillery. At the same time it must be remembered that there was a large force under Wukassovich and Loudon in his rear, and that the Austrians held many strong places in Piedmont and Lombardy. He had to provide for the safety of his flanks and of his communications. It is possible that this could have been done with reduced forces.

His line of communication was precarious, and required strong protection from every direction. The decisive effect of a battle which severed the enemy's line of communication is evident in this campaign

Napoleon's detachment of Desaix with Boudet's division on the eve of battle appeared in the result to be a violation of the principle so frequently enunciated by himself. But the matter has to be regarded in the light of the situation as it presented itself to him on the 13th June. Certainly his assumptions proved wrong, but indications had led him to suppose that Melas did not intend to fight at Marengo, and that he was evacuating Alessandria ; in the light of this assumption, supported by reports from the front of the army, he was obliged to watch his flank towards Novi with a force sufficient to check for a time any Austrian advance in that direction. His other flank, on the north bank of the Po, was similarly protected by Chabran's division. The event illustrates the necessity for thorough reconnaissance to make sure of the enemy's dispositions before adopting any plan, and particularly a plan involving the division of one's forces.

In his "Memoirs," dictated at St Helena, Napoleon indicated three courses which were open to the Austrians. One was to take advantage of their superior numbers to attack and overthrow the French. Or, to cross the Po above Casale, and hasten by forced marches over the Ticino, destroy the French detachments in Lombardy, and reach the line of the Adda. The third plan—to march on Genoa by way of Novi, and await there the expected arrival of a British force from Genoa before resuming the offensive. He appears to have been under the impression, on the 13th June, that Melas was attempting to avoid battle.

It may be observed that had Napoleon been defeated at Marengo, the result would not have been disastrous to him as it was to his adversary. His line of retreat through Stradella and across the Po was open. As he retired he would have received accessions of strength which would at any rate have enabled him to effect his retreat, even though he might not have been in a position to fight another battle.

It is too commonly said that the tactics of a hundred years ago convey no lessons to us to-day, in view of modifications in armament. But this is not true of tactics in their wider sense. Marengo has much to teach us. Napoleon said: "Great battles are won by artillery"; and the Austrian success in the first part of the battle of Marengo bears out the truth of this dictum, for we find the otherwise almost invincible French infantry unable to stand against the Austrian guns.

But, in the final phase of the battle, we see the French succeeding, partly owing to the failure of Zach to make use of his enormous preponderance of artillery, partly also to the faulty formation in which the Austrians advanced. These are, however, negative factors of success. We may, in indicating the causes of the eventual triumph of Napoleon, improve upon his dictum, and say that great battles are won by a harmonious combination of the action of the three arms. Marengo was won by the fierce attack of Desaix's infantry; by the devastating fire of Marmont's guns; by the irresistible charge of Kellermann's cavalry.

Attempts have been made to refer victory to one or other of these factors. It has been ascribed to Desaix, that brave and skilful soldier who arrived so opportunely on the field of battle, who fell in the hour of victory, and of whom Berthier said: "There is the man whom the Orient saluted with the name of the Just, his country with the name of the Brave, his age with the name of the Wise; and whom Napoleon has honoured with a monument." It has been claimed by Kellermann, whose charge cut the leading Austrian column to pieces; it may have been due to the guns which opened a bloody way for Kellermann's horsemen

But the line of battle was reformed·by Napoleon; Desaix's troops were recalled by Napoleon; Kellermann's charge was ordered by Napoleon, who disposed the French batteries. All these gallant men down to the last grenadier, not forgetting the artillery subaltern who, when his leg was shot off, called out to a passing staff officer to be so kind as to tell his gunners to fire a little lower — all performed their part and merited some of the laurels of victory

But success was due, first and last, to the towering genius of the Great Commander, who checked and inspired the retreating troops, who formed the new line of battle, whose clear vision saw light where lesser men would have perceived nothing but darkness, whose calm courage and indomitable spirit turned defeat into victory.

GEORGE ALLEN & UNWIN LTD
LONDON: 40 MUSEUM STREET, W.C.1
CAPE TOWN: 73 ST. GEORGE'S STREET
SYDNEY, N.S.W.: WYNYARD SQUARE
AUCKLAND, N.Z.: 41 ALBERT STREET
TORONTO, 91 WELLINGTON STREET, WEST